Mathematics
Assessment

A PRACTICAL

Handbook

FOR GRADES 9–12

CLASSROOM ASSESSMENT
FOR SCHOOL MATHEMATICS

K–12 SERIES ▪

Edited by

William S. Bush

Anja S. Greer

Grades 9–12 Writing Team

Helen L. Compton

Alice B. Foster

Anja S. Greer

Jo Ann Mosier

Lew Romagnano

Carmen Rubino

Mathematics Assessment

A PRACTICAL

Handbook

FOR GRADES 9–12

NATIONAL COUNCIL OF
TEACHERS OF MATHEMATICS

Copyright © 1999 by

THE NATIONAL OF COUNCIL OF TEACHERS OF MATHEMATICS, INC.

1906 Association Drive, Reston, VA 20191-1502

(703) 620-9840; (800) 235-7566; www.nctm.org

All rights reserved

Third printing 2004

Library of Congress Cataloging-in-Publication Data

Mathematics assessment : a practical handbook for grades 9–12 / edited by William S.
Bush, Anja S. Greer ; grades 9–12 writing team Helen L. Compton ... [et al.].
        p. cm. — (Assessment standards for school mathematics K–12)
    Includes bibliographical references and index.
    ISBN 0-87353-476-X
        1. Mathematics—Study and teaching (Secondary)—United States—Evaluation. I. Series.
II. Bush, William S. III. Greer, Anja S. IV. Compton, Helen L.

QA13 .M153 1999
510¢.71¢273 21—dc21

                                                                            99-045423

Printed in the United States of America

In Memory

We dedicate this book to Anja Greer, who died of cancer during the last stages of its development. She put her heart and soul into this project, but she was not able to see it through to its completion. She contributed a wealth of innovative ideas and tasks, leavened by a keen sense of pragmatism. Her experience and expertise were crucial in shaping this practical resource for teachers.

Anja's passing is a great loss to her family and to her students and colleagues at Exeter and around the country. We mourn her death and with this book celebrate her life.

Table of Contents

ACKNOWLEDGMENTS

We wish to thank the educators listed below for their suggestions, examples, and student work. We applaud their willingness to explore new ways to assess their students and their willingness to share their ideas with us.

Jodi Anderson	Janet Gayheart
Pam Argabrite	Anja Greer
John Barnes	Donna Johns
Charles Beaman	Greta Lawlor
Helen Compton	Cynthia Lawson
Maxine Cox	Karise Mace
Shannon Driskill	Jo Ann Mosier
Donna Farmer	Nancy Nichols
John Fischetti	Robert Ronau
Alice Foster	Carmen Rubino
Sue Fountain	Arlene Smither
Lew Romagnano	Ginny VanHanzinga

Dear Reader,

The National Council of Teachers of Mathematics asked our task force to create an Addenda Series to support the Assessment Standards for School Mathematics. This book, one of six in the series, focuses on assessment in grades 9–12. Three other Practical Handbooks for teachers of grades K–2, 3–5, and 6–8 also contain examples and ideas from teachers who have been successful with assessment. Two Assessment Cases books present descriptions of real classrooms, students, and teachers in assessment situations. They include reflective questions to encourage discussion about important issues in assessment.

The Assessment Standards tells us that classroom assessment should—

- provide a rich variety of mathematical topics and problem situations;

- give students opportunities to investigate problems in many ways;

- question and listen to students;

- look for evidence of learning from many sources;

- expect students to use concepts and procedures effectively in solving problems.

Our collection of examples, reflections, explanations, and tips is intended to help all of us explore this role of assessment in reshaping mathematics teaching and learning. We know that assessment, from simple observations to standardized tests, has always affected what we do in the classroom. We looked for examples that help us do a better job and that allow us to become clearer about what we really want students to learn.

We also know that classrooms and schools are complex environments. Changing assessment practices in nonsupportive environments can be difficult. We will share the experiences and stories of teachers who have had some success.

We must say that we value the role of students in the assessment process—from setting goals to designing and using rubrics to sharing results with others. We feel that students have specific rights while being assessed. We have adapted a list of students' rights developed by Grant Wiggins and included them after this letter. Please read them and think about how they affect classroom assessment.

Many people contributed to this effort. We sought advice from teachers who have been successful with classroom assessment. We found examples of assessment accurately reflecting what teachers believed important and what students were studying and learning. These examples are the most important part of the books.

We hope you will find many uses for this series. Enjoy!

THE ASSESSMENT ADDENDA TASK FORCE

William S. Bush, *Chair*

Charles Allen

Florence Glanfield

Anja S. Greer

Steve Leinwand

Jean Kerr Stenmark

Every student has a right to—

- do interesting work that is useful, challenging, intriguing, or provocative;

- work collaboratively with the teacher to make learning meaningful;

- know the well-defined and clearly stated criteria for assessment or grading;

- be judged according to established criteria rather than her or his rank among competitors;

- get genuine and frequent feedback, both for right now and for long-term progress toward the exit level;

- take part in grading or scoring that will give chances to improve performance, with assessment being recursive and continual;

- have plenty of opportunity to do work of which he or she can be proud, with revisions, self-assessment, and self-correction;

- be able to show, often and in many ways, how well she or he is doing, especially to demonstrate strengths;

- use during assessment whatever resources were available during learning.

Mathematics Assessment: A Practical Handbook for Grades 9–12

Introduction

This is a book about assessment in the secondary school mathematics classroom.

We hope that the information contained in this book will provide you with practical tools and provocative suggestions for classroom assessment. When we use the word *assessment*, we refer to attempts to answer the following questions:

- How can I communicate my expectations about my students' mathematical understanding and the quality of their work?

- What do I think my students understand? What do they think they understand?

- Does the question, task, or activity that I choose raise the mathematical issues I hope it will raise for my students? Does it provide an opportunity for them to show me what they know?

- What question, task, or activity should I use next?

- How can I communicate to my students and others what I think they understand?

We see classroom assessment as the centerpiece of the work teachers do. We know that teachers assess their students continually, both informally (by listening, observing, and interacting with students in class) and formally (through homework, quizzes, tests, and projects).

The ideas in this book come from our own classroom experience, and from the experience of colleagues from around the continent. We have been guided in our work, and in writing this book, by the vision of mathematics curriculum and instruction framed in a series of influential documents, *Curriculum and Evaluation Standards for School Mathematics* (National Council of Teachers of Mathematics [NCTM] 1989), *Professional Standards for Teaching Mathematics* (NCTM 1991), *Measuring What Counts: A Conceptual Guide for Mathematics Assessment* (Mathematical Sciences Education Board [MSEB] 1993), and in particular by these standards taken from *Assessment Standards for School Mathematics* (NCTM 1995):

Standard 1: Assessment should enhance mathematics learning.

Standard 2: Assessment should promote equity.

Standard 3: Assessment should be an open process.

Standard 4: Assessment should promote valid inferences about mathematics learning.

Standard 5: Assessment should be a coherent process.

We have organized our presentation into four chapters. In the first, we set the stage by making the case for considering new ways to assess students. The second chapter focuses on assessment tasks; specifically, how to find, modify, and create them. In the third chapter, we offer ways to plan and conduct a coherent classroom assessment program. We conclude the book with a discussion of scoring, grading, reporting, and using the assessment data we collect.

Each chapter contains these features:

- **Teacher-to-Teacher** and **Student-to-Teacher** letters

- Definitions of common terms (e.g., *open-ended task, analytic rubric*)

- **Tips from Teachers**

- Examples of tasks, student work, rubrics, and strategies for scoring and grading

- Responses to frequently asked questions

- References to primary sources

- References to the accompanying case books

We believe that all students are capable of developing mathematical power. We also believe that how we assess students affects their development in fundamental ways. We hope this guidebook and its companion case book provide you with the practical suggestions that you need. We also hope they provoke you to think about assessment in new ways and that they stimulate discussion among you, your students, and your colleagues about this crucial aspect of the work of teachers.

Why Change? Change What? How Do I Get Started?

I have always considered myself an effective teacher. Over the past few years everything seems to have changed and I need to change to keep up. Text-books now include new topics, and new ways to do the familiar ones. The approaches I've used successfully for years no longer get the same results. I keep hearing about "alternative assessment," "assessment blended with instruction," "student self-assessment," and "mathematics portfolios." What are the benefits of these new approaches over what I do now? Where do I get information about specific ideas, ideas that work with kids?

I have just started teaching high school mathematics. In my college mathematics methods courses, we studied the NCTM Standards books. I learned about different ways to assess students. As this year has gone on, however, I have found that it is hard to try new things on my own. Where do I go for ideas and support?

Changing Assessment Practices

WHY CHANGE MY ASSESSMENT PRACTICES?

Mathematics teaching is more challenging now than it has ever been. Students in mathematics classrooms reflect the population's growing diversity, and the world they live in is changing more rapidly all the time. It is impossible to predict what mathematical knowledge students will need in their lives. They will, however, surely need a connected and conceptual under-standing of a much wider range of mathematical "big ideas." These ideas include number, algebra and functions, data analysis and probability, geometry and measurement, and discrete mathematics.

Through research, we know more now than ever before about how students learn mathematics. The tools now available for teaching and learning were unimaginable even a few years ago.

It is against these new challenges that we pose the question, "Why should we change the ways in which we assess our students?" Much has been written in response to this question. Below are just a few samples:

We must ensure that tests measure what is of value, not just what is easy to test. If we want students to investigate, explore, and discover, assessment must not measure just mimicry mathematics (Mathematical Sciences Education Board 1989, p. 70).

Traditional multiple-choice questions may have a place in mathematics assessment, but they are inadequate for assessing many of our new goals (Stenmark 1991, p. 6).

In a world where we truly believe that ALL students can be successful and where ALL students can and must learn mathematics, traditional assess-ment practices that sort, rank, and stigmatize have less and less value (Stenmark 1991, p. 6).

Students' attitudes, behaviors, and oral and written communication skills must be assessed to provide a complete picture (Stenmark 1991, p. 9).

Frequently we assess to no purpose; collecting information we already possess, do not need, or information upon which we will never act (Clarke 1988, p. 1).

New emphases on mathematical modeling and problem solving, for instance, demand assessment strategies sensitive to process rather than product (Clarke 1988, p. 1).

To be useful to society, assessment must advance education, not merely record its status (Mathematical Sciences Education Board 1993, p. 1).

To be effective as part of the educational process, assessment should be seen as an integral part of learning and teaching rather than as the culmi-nation of the process (Mathematical Sciences Education Board 1993, p. 6).

We have been wrestling with the question "Why change?" for some time. As we examined our own practices and discussed assessment with colleagues, several answers to this question emerged for us:

- Many of our students saw assessment as somehow different from instruction, as a sequence of separate events that were not connected very well with what they did in class each day.

- The approaches we used did not involve many of our students in the assessment process and did not elicit their very best work.

- We were not getting the full picture of the developing mathematical understandings and dispositions of many of our students.

We found that the "Major Shifts in Assessment Practice" in **figure 1.1** captured how our assessment practices needed to change. They provide a vision of how assessment might look in our classrooms. If our classroom assessment is to support the development of mathematical power in all of our students, our assessment practices must undergo many of these shifts.

At this point you may be wondering, "So just how do I 'align assessment with curriculum and instruction' or 'base inferences on multiple sources of evidence'? Where do I begin? How do I know if what I've tried is any better than what I was doing before? Even small changes in practice can have significant—and sometimes unanticipated—effects."

One way to manage changes like those implied by the list of shifts in **figure 1.1** is to plan for assessment in the same careful way that we plan a course, a unit, or a lesson. In the next section we offer some suggestions for assessment planning.

Chapter Overview

In this chapter you will read about—

☐ **the case for changing current assessment practice;**

☐ **planning for assessment;**

☐ **aligning curriculum, instruction, and assessment;**

☐ **strategies for getting started.**

READ ABOUT...

■ *Read about a teacher who wants to change her assessment practices in* "A Scoring Dilemma" in Mathematics Assessment: Cases and Discussion Questions for Grades 6–12 *(Bush 1999).*

FIG. 1.1

MAJOR SHIFTS IN ASSESSMENT PRACTICE (from National Council of Teachers of Mathematics [NCTM] 1995, p. 83)

TOWARD	AWAY FROM
■ Assessing students' full mathematical power	■ Assessing only students' knowledge of specific facts and isolated skills
■ Comparing students' performance with established criteria	■ Comparing students' performance with that of other students
■ Giving support to teachers and credence to their informed judgement	■ Designing teacher-proof assessment systems
■ Making the assessment process public, participatory, and dynamic	■ Making the assessment process secret, exclusive, and fixed
■ Giving students multiple opportunities to demonstrate their full mathematical power	■ Restricting students to a single way of demonstrating their mathematical knowledge
■ Developing a shared vision of what to assess and how to do it	■ Developing assessment by oneself
■ Using assessment results to ensure that all students have the opportunity to achieve their potential	■ Using assessment to filter and select students out of the opportunities to learn mathematics
■ Aligning assessment with curriculum and instruction	■ Treating assessment as independent of curriculum or instruction
■ Basing inferences on multiple sources of evidence	■ Basing inferences on restricted or single sources of evidence
■ Viewing students as active participants in the assessment process	■ Viewing students as the objects of assessment
■ Regarding assessment as continual and recursive	■ Regarding assessment as sporadic and conclusive
■ Holding all concerned with mathematics learning accountable for assessment results	■ Holding only a few accountable for assessment results

Planning for Assessment

HOW DO I PLAN FOR EFFECTIVE AND USEFUL ASSESSMENT?

With the many challenges faced by mathematics teachers today, making the shifts in assessment practices outlined in the last section can seem overwhelming. It has been helpful to us to keep in mind why we spend so much time and energy on assessment. The purposes of assessment are—

- to document students' learning of mathematics;

- to communicate information and expectations to students, parents, other teachers, counselors, colleges, and employers;

- to guide, improve, and provide further opportunities for instruction.

This is the "why" of assessment; what about the "how"? We offer the following set of questions that can guide the planning of assessment for a class, a unit, or a whole course:

- What are the *mathematical concepts or skills* I am trying to assess?

- What important *learning behaviors* should students have at this time?

- How will I assess *what* my students know and can do mathematically?

- How will I *summarize* and *communicate* what I have learned to this point?

In **figure 1.2** is an example of an assessment plan developed by a teacher preparing for a chapter focusing on parallel and perpendicular lines. Note how this teacher answered the first three questions above in her plan. Also note how the planned assessment aligned with her content goals and learning behaviors.

FIG. 1.2

ASSESSMENT PLAN FOR CHAPTER ON PARALLEL AND PERPENDICULAR LINES

> **Assessment Plan**
>
> **Chapter Name:** Parallel and Perpendicular Lines
>
> **Key Math Concepts:** intersecting lines, parallel lines, skew lines, transversal, interior angles, exterior angles, corresponding angles, locus, perpendicular lines, plane
>
> **Key Math Skills:** finding distances between parallel lines, measuring angles, constructing parallel lines, constructing perpendicular lines
>
> **Important Learning Behaviors:** understand relationships among points, lines, and planes, make conjectures about relationships, prove or disprove conjectures, prove theorems, apply concepts and skills to real situations
>
> **Informal Assessment:** observing group work (making conjectures using Geometer's Sketchpad; proving or disproving conjectures; proving theorems); journal writing (explaining concepts and skills; describing relationships; finding examples outside classroom)
>
> **Formal Assessment:** Quizzes (vocabulary, skills, proofs); chapter test (conjectures, proofs, explanations, applications); project (pictures of real-world examples along with descriptions, justifications and explanations)

CHAPTER *1*

Curriculum, Instruction, and Assessment

HOW DO I DECIDE WHAT I WANT MY STUDENTS TO LEARN?

In *Curriculum and Evaluation Standards for School Mathematics* (National Council of Teachers of Mathematics [NCTM] 1989), *mathematical power* is defined as the confidence to solve mathematical problems and to reason and communicate mathematically. Students who possess such power have a sense of the value of mathematics in their lives.

Mathematics classrooms designed with the goal of developing mathematical power in all students will provide—

■ a rich curriculum of engaging, useful, important mathematical "big ideas";

■ an instructional design that supports learning, applying, and connecting those ideas.

Any assessment scheme that accomplishes the purposes of assessment listed in the previous section will be aligned with both of these aspects of the classroom. The *Standards* provides a strong rationale for this alignment:

> *The degree to which meaningful inferences can be drawn from an assessment depends on the degree to which the assessment methods and tasks are aligned or are in agreement with the curriculum. Little information is produced about students' mastery of curricular topics when the assessment methods and tasks do not reflect curricular goals, objectives and content; the instructional emphases of the mathematics program; or how the material is taught.* (NCTM 1989, p. 193.)

HOW DO I ALIGN ASSESSMENT WITH CURRICULUM?

If "knowing" mathematics is "doing" mathematics (NCTM 1989, p. 7), then students in mathematics classrooms will be doing mathematics—that is, participating in purposeful mathematical activities—all the time. These activities will be keyed to the goals of your course or the content standards adopted by your school, district, or state. They will include both novel problems—situations for which there is no solution method to recall—and activities in which students apply methods learned before. Through doing mathematics, students will draw on prior knowledge and adapt and construct new understandings.

An assessment scheme that is well-aligned with your mathematics curriculum will be built around tasks that are similar (both in content and in structure) to the tasks that make up that curriculum. This well-aligned scheme will enable you to gather evidence over time of students'—

■ knowledge of the big mathematical ideas that are at the heart of the course;

■ ability to make and test conjectures;

■ knowledge of a variety of representations (e.g., graphical, numerical, symbolic) of each idea;

■ ability to draw and justify conclusions orally and in writing;

■ capacity for making connections among mathematical ideas.

SOMETHING TO THINK ABOUT

Ask your colleagues what it means to them to align assessment and instruction. Ask them if aligning instruction and assessment is an important goal. Ask them how they know whether or not they are doing it.

FIG. 1.3

CARTOON ABOUT RETAINING HALF

HE'LL PASS IF HE RETAINS AT LEAST HALF OF IT

Curriculum, Instruction, and Assessment

READ ABOUT...

■ *Read about blending instruction and assessment in "Integrating Assessment and Instruction" by Donald Chambers (1993) and "Linking Instruction and Assessment in the Mathematics Classroom" by Kay Sammons, Beth Kobett, Joan Heiss, and Francis Fennell (1992).*

HOW DO I ALIGN ASSESSMENT WITH INSTRUCTION?

When you plan your lessons around your curriculum, you make decisions about—

■ **CLASS STRUCTURE**—the time you allocate to activities; the way you arrange the room; whether your students will work individually, in small groups, or as one large group; the tools you provide students (e.g., graphing calculators, geoboards, algebra tiles, dynamic geometry software); the homework you assign.

■ **CLASSROOM ENVIRONMENT**—the types of questions you ask and answer; when and how you provide information, clarify an issue, model, lead, or let a student struggle with a difficulty; when and how you attach mathematical notation and language to students' ideas; the ideas you choose to pursue in depth from among the ideas your students offer during a discussion.

An assessment scheme that is well aligned with instruction will be aligned with both the structure and environment of the classroom you design, for example:

■ If students have a variety of tools available for instruction, they will have the same tools available for assessment.

■ If students engage in instructional tasks in a variety of formats (individual or group, in-class or outside of class, orally or in writing), they will be able to provide assessment evidence in the same formats.

■ If students are asked a variety of different types of questions during instruction (e.g., "Why is that true?" "Can you explain that another way?" "Is that always true?" "What would happen if...?" "Have you ever solved a problem like this one before?"), they will be asked the same types of questions during assessment.

Having a picture of what aligned assessment and instruction looks like in our classroom can be helpful. We have found that the classroom videos of teachers in action and stories written by teachers provide excellent examples of how instruction and assessment might be blended. Below are some excellent resources:

■ WGBH Education Foundation (1998) videotapes

■ PBS MATHLINE (1994) videotapes

■ Teachers' cases in Merseth and Karp (in press) and in *Mathematics Assesment: Cases and Discussion Questions for Grades 6–12* (Bush 1999).

CHAPTER *1*

Getting Started

HOW DO I START CHANGING MY ASSESSMENT PRACTICES?

You are convinced that what you are currently doing to assess students is not accomplishing all that you need to accomplish. Furthermore, you are ready to try new strategies that will better align assessment with your curriculum and instructional goals. How do you get started? The box on the right contains some tips from teachers who have taken the first steps down the road to changing their assessment practice.

These tips are just a few of many possible first steps you could take. The less familiar the step, the messier and more unpredictable are the results. And the more unpredictable the results, the riskier the first step seems. Whatever steps you choose to take, the following suggestions might make them more manageable and less risky.

Take your first step in the context of a very familiar mathematical topic. Good assessment tasks elicit rich responses from students. The more comfortable you are with the mathematical topic, the easier it will be for you to interpret the evidence students provide. You will be better able to identify novel approaches to problems and recognize deep insights into the mathematics. You will also be better able to diagnose incomplete or unproductive ideas and strategies.

Start with a mathematical topic you are sure needs better assessment. If you are already convinced that your current approach to assessing a topic is not giving you what you need, it will be easier to try something new. It will also be easier for you to judge the effectiveness of the new approach compared to what you were doing.

Observe and interview a colleague who has already taken the step you are considering. With such a colleague, you can examine and discuss the potential effects of that change. You can observe other teachers on videotape. For example, the video cases entitled "Ferris Wheel" and "Group Test," from the *WGBH Assessment Library for Grades K–12* (1998), portray two teachers trying different assessments in their classes. View these tapes and reflect on the strategies you observe and how they play out in these classes.

Work with a colleague who will take the first step with you. One of the most powerful professional development experiences is working with a colleague on a problem of teaching practice. If you take a first step toward changing assessment with a colleague, you will collect more information about its effects. You will also have twice as much analytic power to bring to bear on making sense of this information and deciding what to do next.

Take one step at a time, changing your practice gradually and incrementally. This might seem like common sense, but we are surprised at how often we have tried to do too much too quickly. Each small change helps to define one portion of your overall assessment scheme. By reflecting on each step in light of the purposes of assessment, subsequent steps become clearer and come more quickly.

TIPS FROM TEACHERS

■ *I ask my students "Why?" "How do you know?" or "Can you explain what you did?" as often as possible.*

■ *I ask students to reflect, in writing, on the current mathematical topic or on the day's lesson.*

■ *I pick a particular topic or issue to monitor and document during one or two class meetings.*

■ *I share samples of student work with the class as much as possible.*

■ *I gather student work into small collections that span a period of time.*

READ ABOUT...

■ *Read about getting started with new types of assessment in "Begin Mathematics Class with Writing" by L. Diane Miller (1992), "Some Practical Possibilities for Alternative Assessment" and "Aligning Assessment with the NCTM's Curriculum Standards" by Cathy Schloemer (1993), and "Descriptive-Paragraph Miniproject" by Cherlyn Kern (1997).*

Chapter 2

How Do I Find Out What My Students Know and Can Do?

Teacher-to-Teacher

I have been teaching algebra for ten years now, and I consider myself a pretty good teacher. I have realized in recent years that I really don't know what my students know about algebra. I know which ones struggle with it, and I know which ones find it very easy, but I don't know what they really understand or what they really think about when they solve problems. My weekly quizzes, chapter tests, and homework assignments just do not give me the complete picture. I'm ready to find out what my students really know and can do mathematically, but I am not sure what to do. I really don't have the resources to get started. What kinds of questions and tasks can I give them to challenge them? How can I find out how they think about problems? How I can I find out what they really understand and don't understand? Where can I go to find the tasks and strategies to help me answer these questions? How can I learn to develop my own tasks?

Tools for Assessment

WHAT STUDENT QUALITIES SHOULD I ASSESS IN MY MATHEMATICS CLASS?

As we mentioned in chapter 1, to develop mathematical power our students should—

- understand mathematical concepts and relationships;
- understand and become proficient with mathematical skills;
- be able to reason, justify, and make inferences, both orally and in writing;
- solve problems of all kinds;
- develop positive attitudes and dispositions toward mathematics.

To assess our students' mathematical power fully, we need assessment tools that provide evidence of these qualities. For example, if we wish to assess how well our students understand mathematical concepts, we might ask them to—

- give a definition in their own words;
- give examples and nonexamples of the concepts;
- use the concept in different ways to solve problems.

If we wish to assess how well our students understand and can perform skills, we might ask them to—

- perform the skill at least one way;
- perform the skill in more than one way;
- create a procedure for the skill;
- explain how the skill works;
- explain why the skill works;
- use the skill in different ways to solve problems.

If we wish to assess how well our students can reason deductively we might ask them to—

- justify a mathematical conjecture;
- give examples that illustrate a conjecture, axiom, or theorem;
- give counterexamples of a conjecture;
- complete the missing steps in the proof of a theorem;
- explain how they might prove a theorem;
- explain how they proved a theorem.

If we wish to assess how our students feel about mathematics, we might ask them these questions:

- What is mathematics?
- How do you feel about the mathematics you did today?
- What is your favorite thing to do in math class?
- What is your least favorite thing to do in math class?

If we wish to assess how well our students solve mathematical problems, we might use the criteria listed in **figure 2.1**.

FIG. 2.1

PROBLEM-SOLVING CRITERIA

Your solution will be graded on the basis of the following quintuple of numbers (2, 2, 2, 2, 2) for a total of 10 possible points on each problem.

UNDERSTANDING OF PROBLEM:

2: Complete understanding of the problem is illustrated by choice of models, or diagrams to reframe problem

1: Part of the problem misunderstood – weak choice of way to represent the problem

0: Little evidence of understanding

CHOOSING A STRATEGY:

2: Chooses a correct strategy that could lead to a correct solution

1: Chooses a strategy that could possibly lead to a solution but route has many pitfalls or is inefficient

0: Inappropriate strategy choosen

IMPLEMENTING A STRATEGY:

2: Implements a correct strategy with minor errors or no errors

1: Implements a partly-correct strategy, or chooses a correct strategy but implements it poorly

0: Poor strategy with poor implementation, or correct strategy with no implementation

COMMUNICATION:

2: The justification is well expressed using proper math notation

1: Little justification – math notation poor

0: No justification

OVERALL QUALITY OF PRESENTATION:

2: Attractive, neat, clear, easy for reader to follow

1: Work suggests hasty assemblage with little care for ease in reading or understandability

0: Too much of the work hard to read or follow

From *Problem Solving Strategies: Crossing the River with Dogs*, by Ted Herr and Ken Johnson (1994)

Our assessment tools must capture all of these aspects of student thinking to be effective.

Chapter Overview

In this chapter you will read about—

☐ selecting different tools for assessment:

■ closed tasks
■ open-middled tasks
■ open-ended tasks
■ projects
■ teacher notes and checklists
■ student writing and inventories;

☐ finding good assessment tasks;

☐ modifying assessment tasks;

☐ developing assessment tasks from scratch.

Tools for Assessment

FIG. 2.4

**STUDENT WORK—
COMPUTATION/FILL IN THE BLANK**

---

1. Perpendicular lines are lines that form _____ angles.

2. If two angles are supplementary and congruent, then each angle is a _____ angle.

3. All right angles have _____ degrees.

4. If line *AB* is perpendicular to line *CD* at point *O*, then

    a. the measure of angle *AOD* is _____.

    b. the measure of angle *DOB* is _____.

    c. the measure of angle *COB* is _____.

    d. the measure of angle *AOC* is _____.

WHAT TYPES OF TOOLS FOR ASSESSMENT CAN I USE?

Just as doctors need an array of instruments—thermometers, stethoscopes, X rays, ultrasound, CAT scans—to diagnose our health, we need an array of tools to assess our students' complex mathematical understanding. In the sections that follow, we will describe these tools, discuss advantages and disadvantages of each, and indicate where you can find out more about them.

Closed Tasks

WHAT ARE CLOSED TASKS?

Closed assessment tasks ask students to provide one correct answer. Usually there is only one correct way to reach that answer. Fill-in-the-blank and simple computational tasks like the ones in **figure 2.2** are good examples.

Most true-false and multiple choice tasks are closed. In the examples in **figure 2.3**, there is clearly only one right answer and most students will use memorized facts or procedures to get an answer.

FIG. 2.3

STUDENT WORK—TRUE-FALSE/MULTIPLE CHOICE

1. True or False. Not all negative numbers have square roots.

2. True or False. Every real number is also a complex number.

3. Which of the following is not a quadratic equation?

    a. $y = 2x^2$ **b.** $xy = 16$ **c.** $x^2 - y^2 = 1$ **d.** $y = 3x$

4. The quadratic formula is—

    a. a theorem   **b.** an axiom   **c.** a definition

5. Which is not a square root of –16?

    a. $-4i$ **b.** $4i$ **c.** -4

WHAT ARE THEY GOOD FOR?

Responses to closed tasks tells us whether or not our students can perform a skill or have learned a definition or fact. These tasks are effective in assessing skill proficiency and memorization of important information. They are limited, however, in assessing understanding and problem solving. The one-answer responses to closed tasks do not indicate how students arrived at the response. Furthermore, we do not know whether students thought deeply about the task or whether they simply made a guess.

CHAPTER 2

Open-Middled Tasks

WHAT ARE OPEN-MIDDLED TASKS?

Open-middled tasks, like closed tasks, require one correct answer; however, students may provide different paths to the answer. The student work in **figures 2.4** and **2.5** shows how two students arrived at the same correct answer using two different approaches. In particular, note the differences in their reasoning for part d.

FIG. 2.4

STUDENT WORK—KIRIS FREE THROW 1

3. Twenty people took part in a basketball free throw competition. The first shooter scored 20 points, the second shooter scored 28 points, the third shooter scored the average of the number of points scored by the first two shooters, and each of the next shooters scored the average of all the previous shooters.

a. How many points did the fourth shooter score?

b. How many points did the sixth shooter score?

c. If the first shooter scored **X** points and the second shooter scored **Y** points, how many did the 20th shooter score?

d. How would the results in this problem be changed if the fourth shooter were the first to score the average of all the previous shooters? Explain your reasoning.

BE SURE TO LABEL YOUR RESPONSES (a), (b), (c), AND (d).

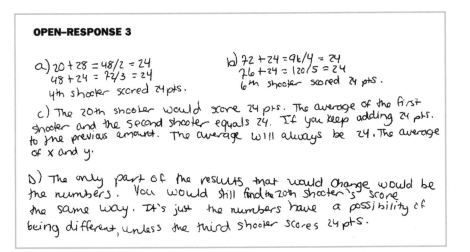

1994–95 KIRIS Common Open-Response Item. Reprinted with permission from the Kentucky Department of Education. Note that KIRIS has been replaced by the Commonwealth Accountability Testing System.

Open-Middled Tasks

FIG. 2.5

STUDENT WORK—KIRIS FREE THROW 2

3. Twenty people took part in a basketball free throw competition. The first shooter scored 20 points, the second shooter scored 28 points, the third shooter scored the average of the number of points scored by the first two shooters, and each of the next shooters scored the average of all the previous shooters.

a. How many points did the fourth shooter score?

b. How many points did the sixth shooter score?

c. If the first shooter scored **X** points and the second shooter scored **Y** points, how many didi the 20th shooter score?

d. How would the results in this problem be changed if the fourth shooter were the first to score the average of all the previous shooters? Explain your reasoning.

BE SURE TO LABEL YOUR RESPONSES (a), (b), (c), AND (d).

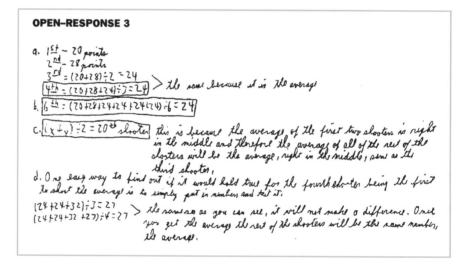

1994–95 KIRIS Common Open-Response Item. Reprinted with permission from the Kentucky Department of Education. Note that KIRIS has been replaced by the Commonwealth Accountability Testing System.

Open-Middled Tasks

True-false tasks can be open-middled when they require students to explain their answers. Look at the examples in **figure 2.6** and compare them to the closed tasks in **figure 2.3**.

FIG. 2.6

STUDENT WORK—TRUE-FALSE/MULTIPLE CHOICE OPEN-MIDDLED

Determine whether the following statements are true or false. If true, prove the statement. If false, provide a counterexample.

1. Every parabola that has an equation of the form $y = ax^2 + bx + c$ has both an x-intercept and a y-intercept.

2. Because of their symmetry, parabolas always have two x-intercepts.

3. If a quadratic equation has one irrational root, it will have two irrational roots.

4. A quadratic equation may have one imaginary root and one real root.

WHAT ARE THEY GOOD FOR?

Open-middled tasks are effective in assessing how students solve problems and think about mathematics. They reveal student thinking throughout the solving process. They give students the opportunity to develop and use their own strategies and to solve problems in ways that are most comfortable to them.

Open-Ended Tasks

WHAT ARE OPEN-ENDED TASKS?

Open-ended assessment tasks have many correct answers and many routes to getting those answers. They include tasks that require students to explain answers, solve nonroutine problems, make conjectures, justify their answers, and make predictions. Students use different strategies for constructing their responses. Note how different the student responses in **figures 2.7** and **2.8** are. Both responses are mathematically correct; however, the first student places his answer in a more realistic and specific context.

FIG. 2.7

STUDENT WORK—KIRIS HOUSE GRAPH 1

4. The graphs below relate the change in the value of a house over time. Explain what could be the reason(s) the value of the house changed as it did for a) <u>and</u> for b).

OPEN-RESPONSE 4

a) In this problem, the value of the house Originally is high, but over time (say a big company laid many people off) due to the # of people w/no jobs. or homes. They all moved out leaving a low value of the house. Then (like in the east end of Louisville now) Many buildings for work open, and people pour into town causing more demand, and the price raises.

b) This is simply something small, dramaticlly changing to something large. Let's say it starts o↳ In 1986. The mayor wants a reconstruction plan to attract home buyers. The city then sets up resturants, clubs, etc... Many homes are built, and by 1996 you have a preatly populated. town, and since every one wants to live there, the demand will be real high and house cost will raise.

1991–92 KIRIS Common Open-Response Item. Reprinted with permission from the Kentucky Department of Education. Note that KIRIS has been replaced by the Commonwealth Accountability Testing System.

Open-Ended Tasks

FIG. 2.8

STUDENT WORK—KIRIS HOUSE GRAPH 2

4. The graphs below relate the change in the value of a house over time. Explain what could be the reason(s) the value of the house changed as it did for a) <u>and</u> for b).

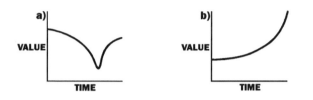

SOMETHING TO THINK ABOUT
Some teachers are concerned about being consistent in scoring tasks with more than one correct answer. How do you determine if all answers and solutions are equally correct? See chapter 4 for a discussion of this issue.

OPEN-RESPONSE 4 A) The time started when the house was built. As time passed on the owners didn't keep up with maintaining the house. So it just kept getting worse and worse. Until one day they decided to fix it up because they were going to sell it. So the value increased back up rapidly.

B) The value of the house started out low. As the owners remodeled and kept up with maintaining the house so the value kept increasing.

1991–92 KIRIS Common Open-Response Item. Reprinted with permission from the Kentucky Department of Education. Note that KIRIS has been replaced by the Commonwealth Accountability Testing System.

The two-part open task in **figure 2.9** clearly illustrates the differences between open-middled and open-ended tasks. The first part of the task, involving painting the pool, is open-middled (it has one correct solution with many routes). The second part requires a report and is open-ended (many solutions and routes).

Open-Ended Tasks

READ ABOUT...

■ *Read about a teacher's concern with presenting a problem that might be too "open" in "Open Car Wash" in* Mathematics Assessment: Cases and Discussion Questions for Grades 6–12 *(Bush 1999).*

■ *Read about a strategy to "open up" closed questions in "Questions with Multiple Answers" by Susan Socha (1991).*

FIG. 2.9

THE PROBLEM POOL

Part I

Your cousin Fred has just built a new swimming pool in his backyard. He has just e-mailed that he desperately needs your help. The water company will be filling the pool three days from now, and Fred still needs to seal it with pool paint. He promised that you'd have use of the pool any time you wish if only you would help him figure how much paint to buy. The paint is very expensive and he doesn't want to buy more than he needs. The pool is rectangular in shape, 20 ft. wide by 40 ft. long. The shallow end is 3 ft. deep. The bottom of the pool is horizontal for 8 ft. and then slants down to a depth of 7 ft. at the deep end. The directions on the paint indicate that a gallon of paint will cover approximately 300 square feet.

Part II

Your cousin Jim, the owner of Jim's Pool Service, received the following letter. As a skilled mathematician and concerned relative, you must advise him on this potentially dangerous situation. Keep in mind that his truck pumps water at 40 cubic feet per minute and that rate cannot be adjusted. Also realize that Jim is an excellent businessman who can understand a well-presented argument.

GOLE CONSTRUCTION AND DESIGN CO.

Dear Sir,

According to our previously arranged contractual agreement, it is time for you to plan for working on the pool at 1234 Heaven View Drive. The swimming pool was built according to the dimensions below:

It will be painted and sealed just prior to your arrival with the water tanker on May 6. The delicately painted sides can be damaged by your water delivery system during the first 12 hours that the paint is exposed to water. Do not add any chemical purifiers until the 12-hour period is over. The water hose should be directed only at the bottom of the pool, not at the painted sides. Also, the rate at which the water level rises cannot exceed 1 inch per minute at and above the 3-foot level (as measured at the deepest end). This is because the curing process takes a while for the painted friezes at the upper levels. I must remind you of our contract that binds you to an agreement accepting full responsibility for any damages. The contract also requires that you make delivery and apply chemical treatment on May 6, directly after the painting and sealing process is completed at 10:00 a.m. that morning. I will be showing the property to a prospective buyer on May 7 at 9:00 a.m. Arrange your schedule accordingly since the contract stipulates a heavy reduction fee unless you finish the job on time.

Sincerely,

L.E. Gole
L.E. Gole

Developed by the teachers of Jessamine County High School in Nicholasville, Kentucky. Reprinted with their permission.

WHAT ARE THEY GOOD FOR?

Open-ended tasks often pose questions based in real situations, thereby giving students a chance to see how mathematics is used outside the classroom. They often require students to make many decisions about using mathematics and sometimes require students to make assumptions and add pertinent information. They provide us with the opportunity to see how our students make problem-solving decisions and how they use the mathematics they have learned. They give students the opportunity to be creative and use their own ideas for solving problems. Students are often motivated to solve open-ended tasks that they generate themselves.

CHAPTER *2*

Projects

WHAT ARE THEY?

Projects are typically extended open-ended tasks. We distinguish them from open-ended tasks because of their length and goals. Projects, like open-ended tasks, have many solutions with many routes to the solutions, but they require many more decisions from students. They generally require students to work for a week, a month, or even a semester. They almost always focus on situations outside school that require students to use mathematics in a variety of ways. They are usually integrated in that they require students to use many different types of mathematics, such as algebra, geometry, or probability in the same task. They connect mathematics to other subjects, such as language arts, science, social studies, art, or music.

An article in *Duke Health* served as a stimulus for an interesting project (see **fig. 2.10**).

The teacher who read this article thought that it would be a good idea to have her students use the data in the article to develop a mathematical model for each of the two estimates given for the rate of incidence of melanoma in the year 2000. The teacher liked the project because of the following:

- The data are given not as numbers of people, but as rates of incidence of the disease, which require students to think about units.

- Few data points were given, leaving open the possibility of a number of basic functions as models.

- The conclusion derived from each model can be tested against information given in the article.

- Technology makes the solution of the problem accessible to most students.

FIG. 2.10

MELANOMA ARTICLE

MELANOMA INCREASE UNDERESTIMATED

The dramatic recent increase in the incidence of melanoma is much greater than reseachers once predicted, according to a report in the *CA–A Cancer Journal for Clinicians*. In 1981, when the risk stood at one in 250, a group of skin cancer experts predicted the risk would rise to one in 150 by the year 2000. However, that level was reached 15 years earlier, in 1985. Currently the risk stands at one in 87. If this trend continues, the risk in the year 2000 will be one in 75. Melanoma incidence is increasing worldwide faster than any other cancer.

Page 12
Duke Health
Winter, 1996

Projects

The teacher next developed the assignment in **figure 2.11**.

FIG. 2.11

MELANOMA ASSIGNMENT

Read the attached article about predictions of incidence of melanoma. Notice that two models were produced to predict the incidence rate in the year 2000. As you investigate the questions below, keep an accurate log of your efforts—what did you try, how did it work, and why was it a good idea. Once you have settled on your best model, answer the following questions:

1. Develop a mathematical model based on the information known in 1981. This model should make the same prediction as developed in 1981 for the rate of melanoma in the year 2000.

2. Develop a mathematical model that uses the currently known data and will produce the prediction of melanoma rate in the year 2000 as 1 in 75.

In the documentation of each model, include—

a. the data used;

b. the method of finding a model—take time to show your methods and include procedures and the analytical support for the results;

c. a graph of the data with model superimposed over the data (be sure scales are labeled);

d. a discussion of why this model is a good model;

e. use of the model to create the year 2000 prediction.

Projects

Figures **2.12** through **2.16** show samples of work from three different students. Note how these students attacked the problem in different ways and how different their solutions are. Also note how students' use of calculators and computers affected their solutions.

FIG. 2.12

STUDENT WORK—MELANOMA #1

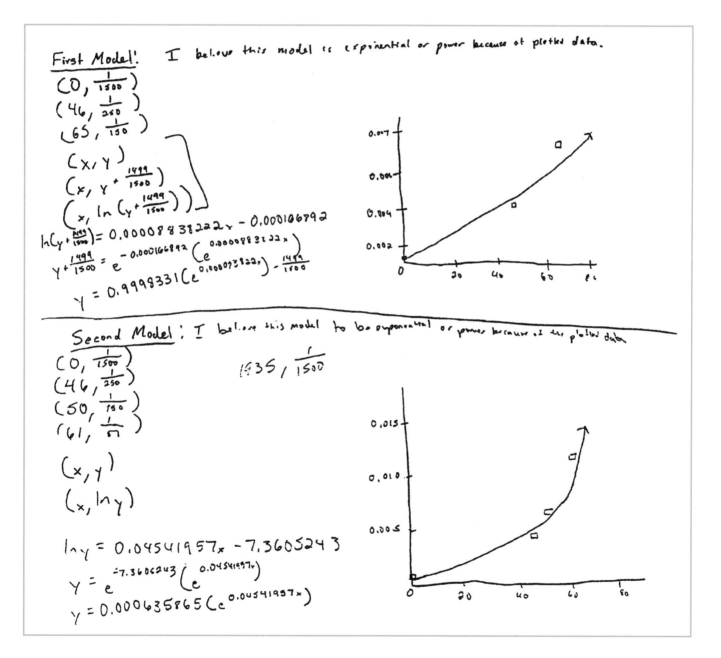

Projects

FIG. 2.13

STUDENT WORK—MELANOMA #2
(ELIZABETH HEALEY)

CPTA-1

Melanoma   Increase Underestimated

From the article there are five points

x	y	
1981	$\frac{1}{250}$	Known
1985	$\frac{1}{150}$	known
1996	$\frac{1}{87}$	known
2000	$\frac{1}{75}$	predicted
2000	$\frac{1}{150}$	predicted (discarded in second)

＊②   ＊first graph points
②
②
②   ②possible second
＊   graph points

For both graphs there is a range restriction of $0 \le y \le 1$. The lowest possible of melanoma is no one having the cancer. The highest possible incidence of melanoma is everyone being affected by the cancer (1 out of every 1 person)

I assume that the first graph with the points $(1981, \frac{1}{250})$ and $(2000, \frac{1}{150})$ is linear. The linear regression line fit to the two points is $1.404 \cdot 10^{-4}x - .2740$

I assume that the second graph with the known three points $(1981, \frac{1}{250})$, $(1985, \frac{1}{150})$, and $(1996, \frac{1}{87})$ is a curve.

Projects

FIG. 2.14

STUDENT WORK—MELANOMA #2
(ELIZABETH HEALEY)

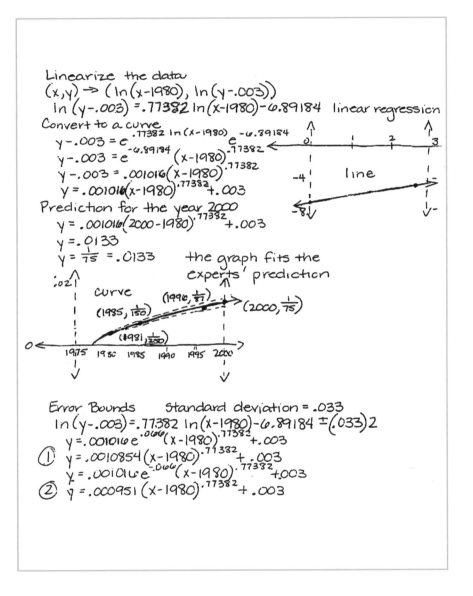

Linearize the data
$(x,y) \rightarrow (\ln(x-1980), \ln(y-.003))$
$\ln(y-.003) = .77382 \ln(x-1980) - 6.89184$ linear regression

Convert to a curve
$y - .003 = e^{.77382 \ln(x-1980) - 6.89184}$
$y - .003 = e^{-6.89184}(x-1980)^{.77382}$
$y - .003 = .001016(x-1980)^{.77382}$
$y = .001016(x-1980)^{.77382} + .003$

Prediction for the year 2000
$y = .001016(2000-1980)^{.77382} + .003$
$y = .0133$
$y = \frac{1}{75} = .0133$ the graph fits the experts' prediction

line

curve
$(1985, \frac{1}{150})$ $(1990, \frac{1}{81})$ $(2000, \frac{1}{75})$
$(1981, \frac{1}{250})$

1975 1980 1985 1990 1995 2000

Error Bounds   Standard deviation = .033
$\ln(y-.003) = .77382 \ln(x-1980) - 6.89184 \pm (.033)2$
$y = .001016 e^{.066}(x-1980)^{.77382} + .003$
① $y = .0010854(x-1980)^{.77382} + .003$
$y = .001016 e^{-.066}(x-1980)^{.77382} + .003$
② $y = .000951(x-1980)^{.77382} + .003$

Projects

FIG. 2.15

STUDENT WORK—MELANOMA #3
(LUCY MELVIN)

Melanoma Problem

In order to better explain my answer for Data Set 1, I am going to show my work for Data Set 2 first.

Data Set 2:
(yrs. since 1980, chance of incidence)
(1, 1/250)
(5, 1/150)
(16, 1/87)
(20, 1/45)

I am including the prediction in my set of data based upon my opinion that the model used to make such a prediction (which is what I am trying to find) would certainly include the prediction.

This is a graph of Data Set 2:

Note that the Data appears very linear. However there may be hidden curviture that we cannot see due to the limitations of our data set.

Through trial and error I found that the best fit results from a Log-Log Linearization. In order to do this most accurately it is necessary to subtract 0.004 from the y-values so that the lowest point in the data set is (1,0). This helps the data fit the format better. However before I take the natural log of both the x values and the y values it is necessary to discard

Projects

FIG. 2.16

STUDENT WORK—MELANOMA #3
(LUCY MELVIN)

READ ABOUT...

■ *Read about a teacher's concern with presenting a problem that might be too "open" in "Open Car Wash" in* Mathematics Assessment: Cases and Discussion Questions for Grades 6–12 *(Bush 1999).*

the point (1,0). This is because you cannot take the natural log of 0. This leaves us with only 3 data points.

(ln x, ln (y-0.004)
Using the data in this format I found the Linear Regression to be:
$$y = (6.2179 \times 10^{-4}) x^{0.5986} + 0.004$$

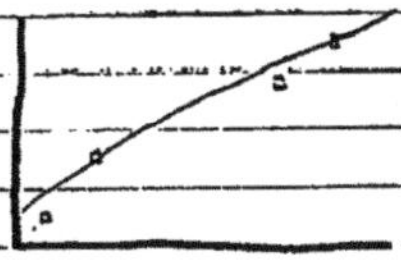

This is very linear, as the graph shows.

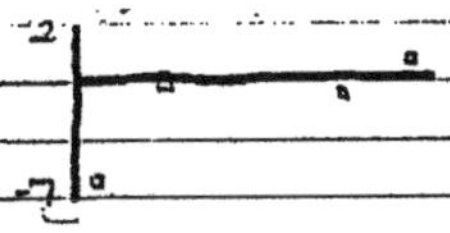

This is the residual plot for this fit. This shows that the fit is good for all but the first point.

Further proof that this is a good fit is that the prediction for 2000 using the model is 0.01325. This compares well with the prediction of 0.0133 made by the scientists. However, extrapolation and interpolation would most likely be bad with this model, because it is only based on 4 points.

Now back to Data Set 1.

There are only two points for Data Set 1:
(1, ½so)
(20, ½so)

Projects

READ ABOUT...

■ *Read more about assessing projects in "Apply the Curriculum Standards with Project Questions" by Richard Edgerton (1993) and in "Assessing Students' Performance on an Extended Problem Solving Task: A Story from a Japanese Classroom" by Yoshinori Shimizu and Diana Lambdin (1997).*

WHAT ARE THEY GOOD FOR?

Projects allow students to see mathematics in action outside the classroom by giving students a chance to connect mathematics with real situations and other subject areas. Projects can be highly motivational. Several students who worked on the melanoma problem wanted to be health-care workers. They were excited about the topic and took great interest in it. These kinds of tasks also require students to make decisions about interpreting information and using appropriate mathematics. They must think about the context of the problem and make decisions that make sense to them. Projects also give students a chance to demonstrate their ability to communicate mathematical ideas either in writing or orally.

Projects lend themselves to group work because they can be broken down into smaller components. They give us, therefore, the opportunity to see how students work together. They also allow us to assess how our students think, how persistent they are, and how they connect ideas. If presentations are part of the assessment, we are able to see how our students communicate mathematics orally.

Projects can be difficult to score. With many different responses possible, some teachers struggle with consistency and objectivity in grading. They are time-consuming for us and our students. Most teachers, however, after noting the excitement and effort that are generated in their students by projects, find the time well spent. They also find that projects were less time-consuming than they expected.

CHAPTER 2

Teacher Notes and Checklists

WHAT ARE THEY?

Teacher notes and checklists are often used during instruction to record evidence from observations or interviews. The evidence may be about individual students or about groups of students. Although notes and checklists are not as formal as tasks, they often yield useful information about students.

Our students usually spend most of their time doing mathematics during daily activities—solving problems, explaining solutions, and asking and answering questions. Most of us recall incidents during class that tell us much about our students, yet few of us collect and record that information in a systematic way. The vignette below tells how one teacher captured some of this important information.

SOMETHING TO THINK ABOUT
It is important that we communicate assessment results to students and parents. How might evidence from notes and checklists be communicated to your students and their parents? How can you use this kind of evidence to shape your teaching? See chapter 4 for further discussion about this issue.

Anne had taken some time during the summer to think about how to assess her students more completely. She decided to assess students' daily work in class and wanted to assess two things:

- *Quality daily discourse—presenting work to the class, offering ideas, responding to the ideas of others, and asking questions*

- *Mathematical insights—comments that help students understand the big ideas in the course*

Anne realized that these goals were general. She wanted to record other behaviors like coming to class on time, being prepared, or paying attention, but she was afraid to try too much. She decided to use a letter code to document students' discourse and insights:

P = quality presentation at the chalkboard. *Q = ask a good question.*

O = offer an idea. *I = share an important insight.*

R = respond to the question or idea of another.

She decided that the seating chart she used for attendance could also be used to record these codes. She made multiple copies and put them on a clipboard. (She also taped a cheat sheet of her five codes at the top.) During class, she carried her clipboard and a pencil. When she observed one of the behaviors, she wrote down the code on the chart.

She labeled five columns in her grade book P, O, R, Q, I. At the end of each grading period, she totaled the codes from her daily charts and recorded a note in the appropriate box for each student. See Anne's grade book in **figure 2.17**.

At the end of the grading period, she had a record of how often each student participated in class and the general type of participation. Throughout the grading period, she met with students to discuss their participation.

FIG. 2.17

ANNE'S GRADE BOOK

NAME	...	P	O	R	Q	I	...
Student 1							
Student 2							
⋮							

Teacher Notes and Checklists

Anne was able to develop a daily assessment scheme because she—

- focused on a single class first;

- analyzed the class's big mathematical ideas;

- used strategies that allowed her to listen to her students;

- developed a short list of valued student behaviors;

- designed a simple set of procedures for documenting student behavior.

Checklists can also be used to record other kinds of student behavior. In **figures 2.18** and **2.19** are two checklists focusing on assessing students as they work in groups. How are these checklists alike and how are they different? Which would you prefer to use when your students work in groups?

FIG. 2.18

CHECKLIST 1 FOR GROUP WORK

Group Checklist

Class:
Grade Level:
Time:
Date:

	Student Name	Task					
Team 1							
Team 2							
Team 3							
Team 4							
Team 5							
Team 6							

CHAPTER *2*

Teacher Notes and Checklists

WHAT ARE THEY GOOD FOR?

Teacher notes and checklists—

- provide a limitless source of information about students' growth, understanding, and disposition;

- communicate to students that we value their daily work in the same way that we value other work;

- provide insights about students whose written work is weak.

When observations are focused and purposeful, we can learn much about our students.

READ ABOUT...

■ *For additional reading about teacher notes and checklists, read "Valuing What We See," by Doug Clarke and Linda Wilson (1994), and* Mathematics Assessment: Myths, Models, Good Questions, and Practical Suggestions, *edited by Jean Stenmark (1991).*

FIG. 2.19

CHECKLIST 2 FOR GROUP WORK

GROUP ASSESSMENT

My group used the following tools in our work:

_____ Pictures or drawings

_____ Graphs

_____ Tables

_____ Measuring tools

_____ Computers

_____ Scientific calculators

_____ Graphing calculators

My group used the following to explain our work:

_____ Appropriate and correct computations

_____ Appropriate and correct mathematical language and terminology

_____ A mathematical model (physical model, picture, equations)

_____ Double checking our result or solution

My group used the following to communicate our thinking:

_____ Logical arguments or explanations

_____ Clear mathematical vocabulary

Student Writing and Inventories

Teacher-to-Teacher

I want my students to become fluent in the language of mathematics. This means that in addition to being able to manipulate mathematical symbols, they should feel at ease reading, speaking, and writing the language. To give them direct experience with writing, I have them spend between five and ten minutes of every homework assignment writing a brief, clear, and technically accurate summary of the important mathematical ideas discussed in class. I tell my students that they are to use clear English sentences in preparing technical summaries of their work.

We spend some time at the beginning of the course practicing writing, since this type of writing assignment is far from commonplace for most students. We begin by reading some of our writing aloud, giving feedback on clarity, technical accuracy, and conformity with the goals of the assignment. Then I review several days' writing and provide feedback. Within a couple of weeks, almost everyone should be on board, and I can work individually with anyone who is still finding the task formidable. The students' writing is given a grade that affects their final grade. How do my students feel about writing in math class? Some enjoy writing very much; many find it challenging. By the end of the term, almost all agree that it is beneficial.

WHAT IS STUDENT WRITING?

Writing in the mathematics classroom can take many forms. We would like to share two of the most popular.

Spontaneous Reflective Writing

Students may be asked to write reflectively at any time during instruction. We can use reflective writing as a "quick start" at the beginning of class to find out if students are ready for a topic. Below are some questions we might ask students at the beginning of a unit on probability:

- What is probability?
- What do you know about probability?
- What are some examples of probability that you have encountered recently?
- What would you like to know about probability?
- How might knowing more about probability be useful to you?

We might also use reflective writing as an "exit slip" at the end of class to check understanding, connections, and beliefs. Here are some topics we might give students at the end of a lesson on conic sections:

- What did you understand best about conic sections?
- What did you understand least about conic sections?
- Write anything you wish about conic sections.
- Explain how parabolas and hyperbolas are alike and different.

CHAPTER 2

Student Writing and Inventories

Journals

Journal writing requires students to write about mathematics on a regular basis. Most teachers have students write in notebooks and submit their journals for review at regular intervals. Some teachers prefer the structure of specific questions or statements for each entry. **Figure 2.20** is an example of a journal page in which students are asked to respond to the same set of questions for every assignment. Note how the cues from the teacher helped the student think through the problem and communicate her results.

FIG. 2.20

JOURNAL ENTRY

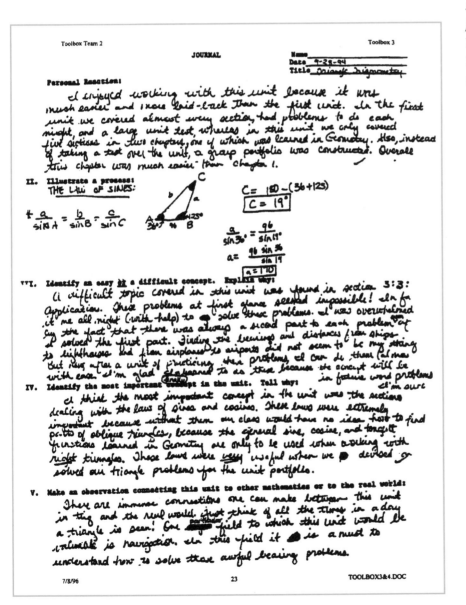

READ ABOUT...

■ *Read more about student writing as a tool for assessment in* Writing to Learn Mathematics, *by Joan Countryman (1992), "Writing: A Necessary Tool for Learning," by Wanda Elliott (1996), "Collaboration and Writing in the Mathematics Classroom," by Adele LeGere (1991), and "No Time for Writing in Your Class?" by Margaret McIntosh (1991).*

■ *Read about a trigonometry teacher's struggle to get students to keep a journal in "Why the Graph Breaks" in* Mathematics Assessment: Cases and Discussion Questions for Grades 6–12 *(Bush 1999).*

Student Writing and Inventories

TIPS FROM TEACHERS

■ *To reduce the volume of writing assignments, ask students to write their comments on index cards and keep the cards in the students' card files.*

SOMETHING TO THINK ABOUT
Some teachers worry that the evidence provided by journal writing and inventories cannot easily be translated into grades or used in grading academic performance. How might teachers use this type of evidence?

The journal questions in **figure 2.21** were designed by a teacher to accompany important homework assignments.

FIG. 2.21

TAKE-HOME JOURNAL ENTRIES

I will look at the following criteria when scoring a take–home journal entry.

1. Did you put some effort into your response? (Reread your response as if you were a teacher who is going to give it a grade.)

    _____ My response shows that I made an effort.

2. Did you communicate your thoughts clearly? (Reread your response a day or so later to see if it makes sense.)

    _____ My response is clear and makes sense.

3. Did you pay attention to spelling, punctuation, sentence structure, etc.? (Reread your response and edit it.)

    _____ I edited my response.

    My response was proofread by _____

4. Is your response complete? (Reread the journal topic and your response to be sure you have responded completely.)

    _____ I checked and my response fits the journal topic.

    My response was checked by _____

WHAT IS STUDENT WRITING GOOD FOR?

Student writing in mathematics class has become a popular tool for assessment for several reasons:

- It gives students a chance to articulate their thinking.

- It increases mathematics learning.

- It helps students view and think about their own accomplishments in mathematics class.

- It gives teachers a chance to detect the depth of our students' understanding and growth in mathematical power and to see exactly what students understand and how they think about solving problems.

- It lets teachers know what students think about mathematics and about themselves.

CHAPTER 2

Student Writing and Inventories

WHAT ARE INVENTORIES?

Inventories allow teachers to learn about students' thinking and beliefs through a checklist. Unlike journals, students write very little in inventories. **Figure 2.22** provides an inventory that asks students to assess their effort and work daily.

The inventory in **figure 2.23** asks students to assess their work over a grading period.

How are these inventories alike and different? Do they assess the kinds of mathematical competencies that you value? Which do you prefer and why?

FIG. 2.22

DAILY SELF–ASSESSMENT INVENTORY

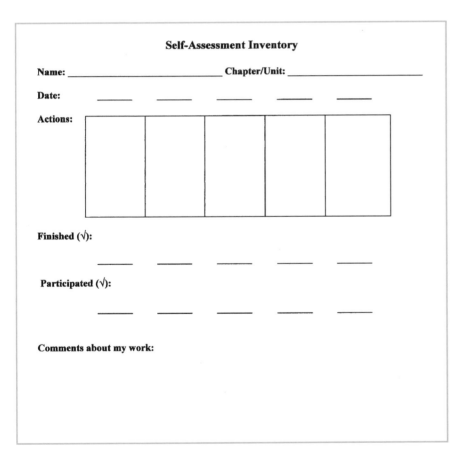

FIG. 2.23

QUARTERLY SELF-ASSESSMENT INVENTORY

SELF–ASSESSMENT REPORT

Select a piece of work or an assignment that represents your best work this grading period. Write a paragraph explaining why it is your best work and what you learned from it. Write another paragraph explaining the key mathematical ideas, concepts, or procedures in the work. Complete the scoring checklist below and turn it in with your two paragraphs.

Name _____

_____ Used tools, physical models, or technology appropriately (3 pts.)

_____ Used graphs, tables, charts, and figures (3 pts.)

_____ Communicated my ideas well by using appropriate vocabulary (3 pts.)

_____ Used mathematics symbols appropriately (3 pts.)

_____ Showed reasoning and logical thinking (3 pts.)

_____ Showed connections among mathematics topics (3 pts.)

_____ Showed connections to topics outside mathematics (3 pts.)

_____ Showed connections to real–world situations (3 pts.)

_____ Total (possible 24 pts.)

Comments about my scoring:

WHAT ARE THEY GOOD FOR?

Inventories, like student writing, provide us some insight into how students think and feel at different times during the year. Although they are not usually as revealing as written responses, they are less time-consuming for both students and teachers. Many teachers have found a combination of writing and inventories the best way to gather evidence.

Summary of Assessment Tools

The chart in **figure 2.24** provides a summary of the tools we have discussed. It identifies the types of student understanding and thinking that the tools best assess. This chart can be helpful in building an assessment program that most effectively uses the many tools of assessment available.

FIG. 2.24

TOOLS-FOR-ASSESSMENT CHART

TOOLS OF ASSESSMENT	EXAMPLES AND REFERENCES	
CLOSED TASKS	● Multiple choice ● True/false items ● Fill in the blanks ● Solve, simplify, graph, …	
OPEN TASKS	● Open-middled tasks (one correct answer with multiple approaches to the solution) ● Open-ended tasks (multiple answers and approaches to the solution)	
PROJECTS	● Short projects ● Extended projects ● Presentation of problem results ● Laboratory activities	
INFORMAL ASSESSMENT	● In-class observations ● Teacher notes and checklists ● Classroom discourse ● Student writing ● Journals ● Conversations	

CHAPTER 2

Summary of Assessment Tools

EVIDENCE OF STUDENTS' UNDERSTANDING/THINKING

- Know "what to do in mathematics"—skills, procedures, and conceptual knowledge
- Use technology
- Use mathematical symbolism and language
- Apply mathematics in a simple context
- Work alone at a given moment

- Apply all the descriptors from the closed tasks
- Know the what and the why in mathematics—using mathematics in different settings
- Solve problems in a mathematical or real-world context
- Use various strategies and justify the strategies
- Organize and interpret information
- Interpret solutions in a more complex setting
- Verify results
- Solve problems and reason
- Use or create mathematical models in order to solve problems
- Communicate thinking
- Connect to prior learning experiences or to mathematical topics
- Work alone and in groups for a short time

- Apply all the descriptors from open tasks to activities that occur over an extended time and that are more complex
- Solve problems and reason while using substantive mathematics
- Revise and be a reflective learner
- Use resources to synthesize information and solve problems
- Demonstrate a disposition to mathematics (e.g., self-confidence, flexibility, persistence, curiosity, use of various tools, enjoyment, valuing both the utility and the beauty of mathematics)

- Develop conceptual understandings (from misunderstandings to sophisticated knowledge)
- Communicate thinking—oral and written
- Draw conclusions, make connections, organize information, revise work
- Question and clarify factors needed to solve the problem
- Demonstrate a disposition toward mathematics (e.g., self-confidence, persistence, use of various tools, enjoyment, valuing both the utility and the beauty of mathematics)
- Apply any of the descriptors from the categories above

Finding and Modifying Good Assessment Tasks

WHAT DO I NEED TO THINK ABOUT IN FINDING NEW TASKS?

Selecting new tasks requires some thought. Poor tasks can waste valuable class time, frustrate our students, or provide misleading information about students. We have found the following questions helpful in thinking about whether tasks are useful:

- *What am I trying to find out?* How well do students understand the concepts? How well do students perform and understand the skills? How well will students use what they learned to solve problems? Can students explain what they know?

- *Why is it important?* Is the concept or skill important in a wide variety of mathematical situations? Do students need to understand the concept in order to learn a new topic? Is it a skill students will frequently be asked to use? Is it an important strategy for solving problems?

- *What are my criteria for success?* Is a correct answer sufficient? Do I expect students to provide more than one correct answer? Do I want students to justify their responses? Do I want students to use a skill or concept in a different situation?

- *How will I use the evidence I get?* Will I make mid-course adjustments? Will I let students know the results? Do I want to know more about my students' thinking? Will I use it to determine a grade? Will I share the results with parents?

 **CHAPTER** 2

Finding and Modifying Good Assessment Tasks

Good assessment tasks can provide a positive instructional experience for students. We can use some of the same criteria for gathering assessment tasks that we use for finding good instructional tasks—that they be engaging, relevant, challenging, and mathematically appropriate. It is important, however, to realize how good assessment tasks differ from good instructional tasks. **Figure 2.25** explains some of these differences.

READ ABOUT...

■ *Read about a calculus teacher's struggle with communicating expectations to students in "Enormous Gulp"* in Mathematics Assessment: Cases and Discussion Questions for Grades 6–12 (Bush 1999).

FIG. 2.25

HOW ASSESSMENT TASKS AND INSTRUCTIONAL TASKS ARE DIFFERENT

Some Differences between Assessment and Instructional Tasks

To be effective and easily scored, assessment tasks must meet some requirements that are not necessary for instructional tasks. Here are some additional tips for constructing assessments.

Avoid ambiguity.

Although ambiguity in instructional tasks allows students a greater range of assumptions and approaches, such ambiguity detracts from an assessment. We want students to know what we want them to accomplish and how they will be judged. A good assessment task makes sense and conveys purpose, even to students who do not fully accomplish that purpose.

Make the purpose clear at the beginning.

In instructional tasks, we may sometimes ask students to do several separate guided activities that are then brought together into a coherent whole. However, in assessments, the students should be made clearly aware of the purpose of the assessment at the beginning, either explicitly through a simple checklist ("This task is to find out if you can...") or implicitly by clearly worded questions.

Avoid choosing a context merely to provide interest.

Dimensions that add interest in instruction may distract in assessment. The context should make the problem easier, not harder. Eliminate complicated contexts that are not directly related to the mathematics or contexts that are "gimmicks" intended only to provide interest.

Don't try to assess understanding of several concepts at once.

Although the longer tasks should be rich, allowing students to employ a variety of concepts and processes, they should not attempt to assess too many different concepts.

Avoid unnecessary cleverness in prompts.

Often a very straightforward prompt elicits the most creative work from students. A rule of thumb is that the task designer should write fewer words than she expects to get in the student response.

Finding and Modifying Good Assessment Tasks

WHERE CAN I FIND GOOD ASSESSMENT TASKS TO GIVE MY STUDENTS?

Finding good tasks for students is an important step in changing our assessment practices. Good assessment tasks—

- assess a wide range of mathematical knowledge including important concepts and essential skills;

- are well aligned with instruction;

- clearly provide the evidence we seek from students.

Teachers have adopted several strategies to find assessment tasks that meet these criteria. We would like to share some of these strategies and provide good examples.

Look in Professional Journals and Books

Professional journals and books are rich with assessment ideas. The bibliography of this book contains many excellent resources for high school teachers.

Figure 2.26 shares an article written by Gail Burrill (1996) in the *Mathematics Teacher*. It offers an excellent assessment task for students learning about making estimates and judging good estimates.

CHAPTER 2

Finding and Modifying
Good Assessment Tasks

FIG. 2.26

FAMOUS PEOPLE

FAMOUS PEOPLE NAME _____

How well can you estimate the ages of famous people?

1. The following list contains the names of thirteen famous people. Without talking to anyone, write down your estimate of the age of each person. If you do not know the person, make a guess.

ESTIMATED AGE

Nancy Reagan _____

Mister Rogers _____

Sandra Day O'Connor _____

Chelsea Clinton _____

Eddie Murphy _____

Tom Brokaw _____

Roseanne _____

Frank Sinatra _____

Oprah Winfrey _____

Heather Locklear _____

Garth Brooks _____

Jane Fonda _____

Ringo Starr _____

2. Obtain the actual ages from your teacher. How well were you able to estimate the ages of the famous people? To help answer this question, make a scatterplot with your estimate of the age on the horizontal axis and the actual age on the vertical axis.

a) How will you decide if someone is a good estimator of the ages of this group of famous people?

b) Where will a point lie if your estimate is correct? Draw in the line that represents estimates that are 100 percent accurate. Write an equation of the line.

c) What does it mean if a point is above the line? In general, did you overestimate or underestimate? How can you tell?

3. Look at the plots made by others in your group. Decide who is the best estimator among your classmates and give a mathematical reason for your choice. Be ready to defend your process for the rest of the class.

Finding and Modifying Good Assessment Tasks

We study linear data analysis early in the school year. Since working in large and small groups is important to me, I incorporated group work into the activity. The Mathematics Teacher *activity seemed like fun and would be interesting to the kids. I added names to the list—the principal, another teacher, and Mickey Mouse. The greatest conversation was about Mister Rogers. Each student recorded the name of the famous person and the student's estimate of age. Once they gave their estimates, I gave them the correct ages. The assessment followed. The assessment was done in small groups of three or four students. Each group had the data from its group members. Each group also had a composite set of data from the whole class. I asked them to perform the following tasks:*

- *Compare the abilities of your group members to guess the ages of these famous people.*

- *Give a list of instructions about how to use the scatterplot of points to identify the best guesser.*

- *Using the class composite estimates, determine how good we are as a class at estimating the ages of famous people. Write several sentences to describe how you measured our abilities.*

CHAPTER 2

Finding and Modifying
Good Assessment Tasks

Below is an example of how one teacher used the article as an assessment task. Not only did the task allow students to judge their own estimates, but also the ideas developed by students led directly to the concept of best fit. A sample of one pair of students' work can be found in **figure 2.27**. Note the quality of their analysis and their use of technology—talk about developing mathematical power!

FIG. 2.27

STUDENT WORK—FAMOUS PEOPLE'S AGES

FAMOUS PEOPLE NAME _____
MATH CLASS   9/12/97

Our class was given a list of famous people. We had to estimate their ages. We decided to use the best guesses from our papers. We were given the birthdates after we made our guesses.

Famous Person	Our best guess	Real age	Birthdate
Nancy Reagan	75	73	1924
Mister Rogers	55	68	1929
Sandra Day O'Connor	60	67	1930
Chelsea Clinton	17	17	1980
Eddie Murphy	35	36	1961
Tom Brokaw	45	57	1940
Roseanne	40	45	1952
Frank Sinatra	80	82	1915
Oprah Winfrey	41	43	1954
Heather Locklear	31	36	1961
Garth Brooks	37	35	1962
Jane Fonda	50	60	1937
Ringo Starr	45	57	1940

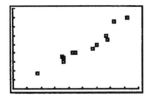

This is a graph of comparing the real age as the x's and our guess as the y's. If we had been right all the time, these points would have lined up along the graph of $y = x$.

Below is a graph of our data with the line $y = x$ on top of it.

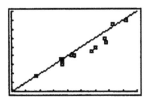

As you can see, we usually guessed the age to be lower than it actually is. We think this is because of all the make–up and face lifts that famous people have.

Finding and Modifying Good Assessment Tasks

Listening to Students

Students can often help us identify the best assessment tasks. They know which ideas need clarification. They can tell the difference between questions that focus on skills and questions that focus on concepts. They also have different views of some concepts and problems. We can get good tasks from our students if we just listen to their comments and questions. Below is a vignette of how one teacher used students' comments and questions to get a good assessment task. Student work is illustrated in **figure 2.28**. In particular, note the language they used to explain their thinking.

My algebra two class was going over homework problems in small groups. One of the problems asked students to graph the equation

$$y = \frac{x^2 - 1}{x}.$$

Two students in one group were arguing about the problem. One rewrote the equation as

$$y = x - \frac{1}{x}.$$

He then began with the graph of y = x and subtracted values of 1/x from the y-value corresponding to each x-value. The other student used the ideas developed in class for graphing rational functions by using asymptotes, zeros, and positive-negative regions of the function. As the students discussed who was right, an idea for an assessment task was born.

I developed the following task:

Two students were each given the equation of a function and asked to put the equation and its graph on the board. Greta got h(x) = x – 1/x and Marcus got g(x) = (x² – 1)/x. As they graphed the functions, they realized that g and h were, in fact, the same function written in different forms. They also noticed that some characteristics of the graph were more easily explained from h than g, while others were more easily explained from g than h. Identify these characteristics and explain why they are more easily seen from one form than the other. Be sure to include both local and global behavior in your explanation. Figure 2.28 provides a sample of student work.

FIG. 2.28

STUDENT WORK—FUNCTION EXPLANATION

From h(x) we can see that, globally, the function will look like y=x because 1/x becomes insignificant as x increases. Also we can see that there will an oblique asymptote at y=x because h(x) can never equal x because 1/x ≠ 0.

From g(x) we can tell that the roots are 1 and -1 because x²-1 in the numerator is factorable to (x+1)(x-1). Also, we can easily tell that x≠0 because it is in the denominator and division by 0 is undefined. We know that the graph will be a hyperbola because the equation is that of a rational function.

Finding and Modifying Good Assessment Tasks

Assessment tasks can also arise during class discussions. The idea for the following assessment task came from a difficulty that a student encountered in class when using a calculator to graph a function.

The graph of $y = 3/(x - 15) + 50$ is shown below [fig. 2.29] using the window $-500 < x < 500$ and $-500 < y < 500$ with marks at every 10 units on each axis.

 The graph looks like a horizontal line. At what y-value is the line located and why?

■ Sketch a graph of this function showing the expected behavior and label important points or features of the curve. Use a variety of windows and scales. (See second graph in figure.)

■ What are the domain and range of the function?

■ What viewing window is appropriate to see the local behavior on the function on your calculator?

FIG. 2.29

GRAPHS OF FUNCTION

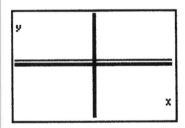
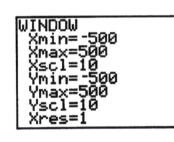

Graph and Window with parameters set at –500 and 500

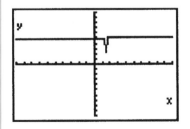

Graph and Window with parameters set at –100 and 100

Finding and Modifying Good Assessment Tasks

FIG. 2.30

STUDENT WORK—CANE TOADS 1

Sydney—In June 1935, Australia imported the South American cane toad in order to control the destructive sugar cane beetle that was threatening the sugar cane crops. However, due to the high growth rate in population because of its rapid reproduction and because of the absence of predators in Australia, the cane toad has taken over Australia.

In June 1935, 101 cane toads were brought to Australia, and in March 1937, the population has grown to 64,543. This was a 34% increase per month and a 3491% increase per year. With these rates, the cane toad population will double in only 2.37 months!

FIG. 2.31

STUDENT WORK—CANE TOADS 2

April 1, 1937

Sydney, Australia—You might be wondering what's up with all these toads hopping around. One hundred and one toads, known as the South American cane toad, were brought to Australia in June 1935. The government brought them to control the spread of the sugar cane beetle that was destroying our sugar cane crops. The toad accomplished its goal; however, at the end of last month, there were 64,543 cane toads. This type of growth is extraordinary and will cause us problems very soon. If this type of growth continues, the toad population will double about every 2 months and 8 days. This means that there will be over a million of those green critters in only 30 months!

Tasks from the News

Newspapers, periodicals, and magazines are full of ideas for assessment tasks, especially tasks involving statistics.

A teacher was intrigued by an article in the October 1990 issue of the *Smithsonian*. The title of the article was "Way Down Under, It's Revenge of the (Yech!) Cane Toads" and it reported incredible growth patterns for cane toads in Australia.

Below is an assessment task created by the teacher from this article.

> I need an article (no more than one page) about the situation described below. The reason I am assigning this article to you is because I know you are a mathematician and can help us forecast our future problems with the cane toad.
>
> Include factual information that our readers will find interesting and your math teacher would find significant. You may include graphs and tables but also give written descriptions.
>
> Topic: Cane Toads in Australia
>
> The cane toad, a native of South America, was introduced to Australia as a method of controlling the destructive sugar cane beetle that threatened the sugar cane crops. Since its introduction in 1935, the cane toad population has exploded to menacing proportions. It has no natural predators in Australia and it reproduces rapidly. There were 101 cane toads brought to Australia in June 1935. In March 1937 the population of cane toads had grown to 64,543.

Figures 2.30 and **2.31** offer two samples of student work from the cane toads task. These students have learned to summarize their findings in succinct ways.

CHAPTER 2

Finding and Modifying
Good Assessment Tasks

Problems from Old Textbooks

Our bookshelves are filled with copies of mathematics textbooks that we no longer use. These books are filled with great ideas for teaching and assessment. Sometimes simply thumbing through them can inspire good ideas. Here is how one teacher used an old textbook (*Solid Geometry* by Shute, Shirk, and Porter [1957, p. 100]) to create an interesting assessment task:

> *We were studying three-dimensional shapes in my geometry class. The ideas were straightforward, but my students were challenged by trying to visualize the shapes. Their self-confidence was waning. I needed an assessment activity that was challenging yet attainable for them. As I looked through a very old geometry book, an illustration caught my eye. It was familiar, but my first reading of the text offered me little help in thinking about a problem. I could relate to my students. I got a box and some string to help me think about the problem. This was just what I was looking for. See **figure 2.32**.*

FIG. 2.32

RIBBON PROBLEM FROM SHUTE, SHIRK, AND PORTER

195. Practical application: Tying gift packages

Gift packages in the shape of rectangular parallelepipeds are often made both attractive and secure by tying them with ribbon of appropriate color and material

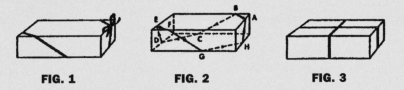

FIG. 1   FIG. 2   FIG. 3

in the pattern shown in Figs. 1 and 2. Assuming the dimensions of the package illustrated are 8 in. by 4 in. by 2 in., the total length of the ribbon, exclusive of decorative bows, is 23.3 in. (Figs. 4 and 5). If the package were tied in the conventional way (Fig. 3), the total length of the ribbon world be 32 in. Because the first pattern is more economical, it is widely used in industry and in commerce in preparing packages of goods for marketing. Many individuals also use this pattern in their gift wrapping.

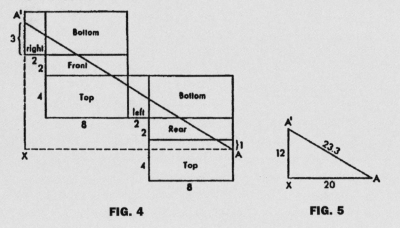

FIG. 4   FIG. 5

Finding and Modifying Good Assessment Tasks

*I transformed the textbook problem into the problem in **figure 2.33** for my students.*

FIG. 2.33

TRANSFORMED PROBLEM FOR ASSESSMENT TASK

2. Given a package (rectangular solid in shape) that is tied with ribbon or cord as shown in the figures. Given that the package is 8 in. by 4 in. by 2 in. and the cord in figure 1 is 23.3 inches in length (excluding the bow) and the cord in figure 3 is 32 inches in length (excluding th ebow). Unfold the box and consider the path of the ribbon (like an ant with ink on his toes that walks the path of the ribbon). Draw a diagram of the unfolded box and show the ribbon for both figures. Are the lengths of ribbon or cord correct? Explain.

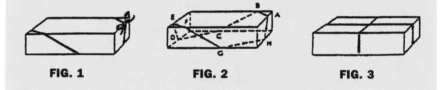

FIG. 1   FIG. 2   FIG. 3

*I placed my students in groups and asked them to give me a written answer in two days. I gave them some time in class to discuss strategies, but I wanted them to spend some time out of class to think about the problem alone. This would also give them a chance to build models if they needed them. **Figure 2.34** provides a sample of student work. This student's visual skills led her to the "surprising" solution.*

Finding and Modifying
Good Assessment Tasks

FIG. 2.34

STUDENT WORK—RIBBON PROBLEM

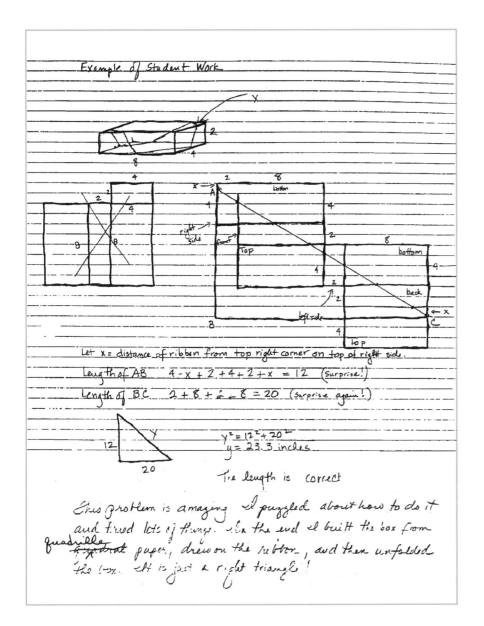

Example of Student Work

Let x = distance of ribbon from top right corner on top of right side.

Length of AB $4 - x + 2 + 4 + 2 + x = 12$ (surprise!)

Length of BC $2 + 8 + 2 + 8 = 20$ (surprise again!)

$y^2 = 12^2 + 20^2$
$y = 23.3$ inches

The length is correct

This problem is amazing. I puzzled about how to do it and tried lots of things. In the end I built the box from quadrille ~~graphed~~ paper, drew on the ribbon, and then unfolded the box. It is just a right triangle!

Finding and Modifying Good Assessment Tasks

Old Quizzes and Tests

Our old quizzes and tests can also provide excellent resources for new assessment tasks. Once we become committed to changing our assessment practices, we can look at old assessments with new eyes. Although many of our good tasks remain good tasks, some tasks need to be modified to meet our new goals for instruction. In the vignette below, read how one teacher transformed a set of old true-false questions to create an open-ended task that elicited more thinking and discussion.

I found the following true-false statements on an old test of mine.

Respond true or false to the following statements:

1. The median of a trapezoid is parallel to the base.

2. Every rectangle is a square.

3. Two parallel lines are equidistant at all points.

4. If a parallelogram has two adjacent sides congruent, then it is a rectangle.

5. The segment that joins the midpoints of two sides of a triangle is parallel to the third side.

I decided to use these statements to stimulate discussions in small groups. Students would have to explain ideas to other students and they could not simply guess. I transformed the instructions for the true-false statements into the following task:

Your group will determine which of the following statements are true and which are false. In your discussions, sketch several figures to illustrate and show relations among shapes. If a statement is false, determine how to modify the statement to make it true. It is not sufficient to just insert a *not* into the statement. After twenty minutes we will have a whole-class discussion of the answers. A group and one member of that group will be selected at random to lead the discussion that will explain one of the statements.

The following year, I revised this task in another way. I had begun to have students explore geometric relationships with Geometer's Sketchpad. I wanted a task that would allow them to incorporate the Sketchpad.

You will determine which of the following statements are true and which are false using Geometer's Sketchpad. In your exploration, construct a figure that fits the requirements of the statement. Be sure every given condition is expressed in the figure. Once the construction is done, attempt to modify the figure by changing the lengths of sides and angle measures and by removing seemingly parallel or perpendicular lines. Notice what kinds of quadrilaterals result. Notice what characteristics cannot be changed.

CHAPTER 2

Finding and Modifying Good Assessment Tasks

In addition to modifying the mathematics content and form of assessment tasks, it may be necessary to modify how the task might be presented to students. **Figure 2.35** provides an example of how to expand a task to meet different assessment goals.

FIG. 2.35

EXPANDING A TASK

READ ABOUT...

■ *For more reading about expanding assessment tasks, read "Polishing a Data Task: Seeing Better Assessment" by Judith Zawojewski (1996).*

Closed Task (10 minutes)

8. A forensic scientist can calculate the height of a murder victim from the lengths of certain bones—the femur, the tibia, the humerus, and the radius. See the figure.

Here are the formulas used if the length of the femur is known:

Male: $h = 69.089 + 2.238F$

Female: $h = 61.412 + 2.317F$

where h is the height in centimeters and F is the length of the femur in centimeters.

a. Find the height of a female victim whose femur is 40 centimeters.

b. Find the height of a male victim whose femur is 49 centimeters.

From Rachlin, Sidney, Annette Matsumoto, and Li Ann Wada. *Algebra I: A Process Approach*, p. 141. Honolulu: University of Hawaii Curriculum Research and Development Group, 1992.

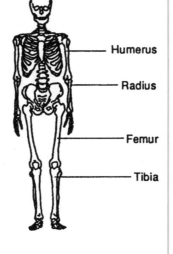

Open-Ended Task (1 hour)

A forensic scientist wants to calculate the height of a murder victim from the length of the victim's femur (thigh bone). Over the years the scientist has compiled the following data about deceased males and females.

Males			Females		
	Femur (cm)	Height (cm)		Femur (cm)	Height (cm)
Subject A	51	183	Subject H	42	156
Subject B	46	173	Subject I	49	175
Subject C	47	178	Subject J	39	147
Subject D	56	193	Subject K	45	168
Subject E	42	165	Subject L	42	160
Subject F	56	198	Subject M	54	183
Subject G	53	185	Subject N	39	152

The scientist would like you to use these data and estimate the height of a male with femur length 49 cm and the height of a female with femur length 44 cm.

Project (2 days)

You are a forensic scientist and believe that a relationship between the height of teenagers and the length of their femurs (thigh bone) exists. Furthermore, you think that the relationship might be different for males and females. Gather data

Developing Assessment Tasks from Scratch

READ ABOUT...

■ *For more reading about designing tasks, read "Assessing Students' Ability to Analyze Data: Reaching beyond Computation" by Frances Curcio and Alice F. Artzt (1996).*

HOW DO I DEVELOP NEW ASSESSMENT TASKS FROM SCRATCH?

Often we cannot find a task or activity that meets our assessment needs, and we must develop a task from scratch. Developing tasks can be fascinating and instructive for both our students and ourselves. Read below how two colleagues developed a task for their students.

I needed an assessment task to determine if my students could interpret graphs. I looked in books, at old questions, and at ideas from the textbook. I found nothing that satisfied me. I talked to a colleague teaching the same class, and she was also looking for a similar task. We talked awhile about our goals for our students. We discussed the activities we had done in class. We made a list of what we wanted students to be able to do. We wanted a task that would require students to defend their answers and allow them some room for interpretation. We decided that the best tasks are those in which students are given a graph and asked to provide a situation that describes the graph. We brainstormed and sketched possible graphs, but nothing satisfied us that day.

*The next day, my colleague was waiting for me at the door. "I think I have an idea," she said. She showed me two graphs. (See **fig. 2.36**.)*

FIG. 2.36

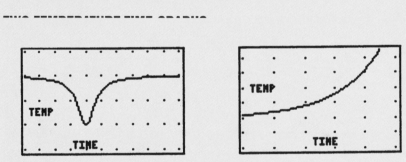

The instructions for the task were as follows:

Graphs A and B show the temperature in an oven over time. Explain what could cause the temperature to change as it did.

I tried the task out myself. It fit the criteria we had set for the task. It was open enough to capture creative ideas from students but structured enough for us to know if students understood.

Preparing Assessment Tasks for Students

HOW DO I PREPARE AN ASSESSMENT TASK FOR STUDENTS?

Once we have found, modified, or developed an assessment task, some work is necessary to prepare it for our students. It is generally not a good idea just to give the task to students and see what happens. The task may not meet or align with our goals, it may be confusing to students, it may discourage students, or it may result in misleading evidence. The flowchart in **figure 2.37** describes how one teacher prepares a task for her students. Note that the process includes many of the steps used by other teachers mentioned in this chapter.

Fig. 2.37

FLOWCHART FOR PREPARING A TASK FOR STUDENTS

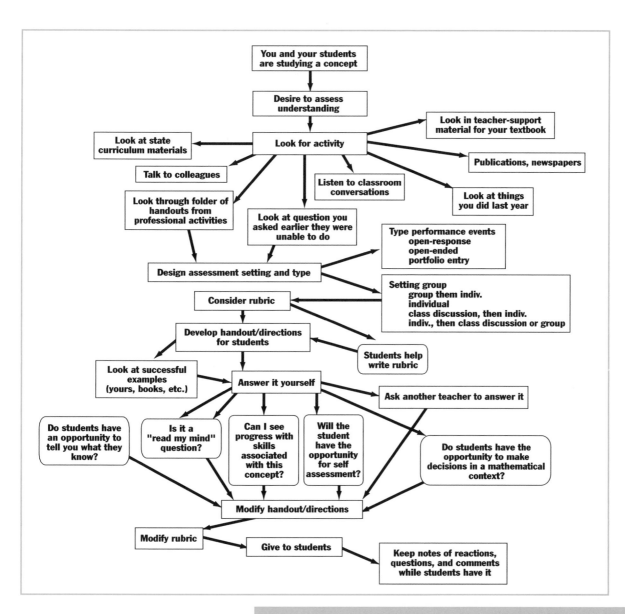

How Do I Put It All Together?

SEE...

■ *See other examples of assessment plans in* **figure 1.6** *in chapter 1 and in* **figure 4.7** *in chapter 4.*

Developing an Assessment Plan

HOW DO I DEVELOP AN OVERALL ASSESSMENT PLAN THAT INCLUDES A VARIETY OF TOOLS?

Before we begin a new class, we develop an instructional plan. This plan helps us keep the big picture in mind and guides our instructional decisions. It is also important that we develop an overall plan for assessment.

Developing such an assessment plan provides a road map to guide and inform us, our students, and their parents, about expectations and performance. Otherwise, we will not be able to capture the variety of mathematical abilities of our students. In addition, we run the risk of assessing unnecessarily and wasting far too much valuable time. To be effective, our assessment must be comprehensive and focused. A good assessment plan will describe our roles as teachers as well as the roles of our students.

An assessment plan might include some or all of the following items:

■ Our unit or lesson goals

■ Mathematics content (minimally the big ideas, maximally a list of topics)

■ Important mathematical assessment targets (e.g., problem solving, group work, oral and written communication, reasoning, applying)

■ List of assessment tools to be used

■ Plans for scoring and feedback

In **figure 3.1** is an assessment plan developed by a high school teacher for an integrated mathematics course. The teacher chose to base the plan on a point system to help with grading. (Some teachers may find that including the points ahead of time is too constraining and might wish to modify them as the marking period progresses.)

The plan clearly communicates to students and others what is expected of the students in the class. Note, however, that the plan does not identify specific course goals nor does it indicate how the accumulated points will transfer into a grade. Some teachers may wish to include these items in their own assessment plan.

FIG. 3.1

ASSESSMENT PLAN

ASSESSMENT PLAN—INTEGRATED MATH LEVEL 2

The following types of assessment will be used to gather evidence about how well you understand and can use the mathematics studied this marking period. The quarter grade will be based on the total number of points you earn.

Test and Quizzes: T points

Purpose	■ *to evaluate students' ability to work independently in a supervised setting*
Evidence	■ *knowledge of, and ability to apply, the big ideas*
	■ *quizzes—understanding conveyed by quick execution of skills or techniques*
	■ *tests—understanding conveyed by selection, execution, and justification of problem-solving strategies*
Frequency	■ *quizzes—several times a week; on limited range of topics*
	■ *tests—four or five a quarter; problems cumulative*
Evaluation	■ *quizzes—point for each correct response*
	■ *tests—analytical scoring per problem*

Group Problem Set: G points

Purpose	■ *to evaluate ability to work collaboratively*
Evidence	■ *problem-solving strategies—communication skills—listening skills*
	■ *creating a finished product by weaving different ideas from several people*
Frequency	■ *at least once a week*
Evaluation	■ *teacher observation checklist—4-point scale*
	■ *self-assessment checklist—4-point scale*

Homework / Daily Participation: H points

Purpose	■ *preparation and thinking for next class—individual practice of skills and techniques*
Evidence	■ *ability to write complete solutions using a variety of resources: notes, text, calculators, computers, peers*
	■ *ability to discuss mathematical ideas—orally/extemporaneously respond to questions from peers*
Frequency	■ *assessed almost daily*
Evaluation	■ *homework when collected on 4-point scale*
	■ *participation based on accumulation of contributions—type of contribution recorded each day*

Special Problem Sets: S points

Purpose	■ *work in a nonsupervised setting on a substantial problem; the problem may well take several days and a couple of drafts to complete—some done with a partner*
Evidence	■ *ability to make connections, see generalizations/patterns, extend problems creatively*
	■ *ability to persist with a nonroutine problem*
	■ *ability to work with a partner over a sustained period of time*
Frequency	■ *once every other week*
Evaluation	■ *4-point scale*

Portfolio: P points

Purpose	■ *reflection of what has been learned*
Evidence	■ *quality and variety of work—growth in understanding—depth of assimilation*
Frequency	■ *once a term, near end of term*
Evaluation	■ *2-point scale: completed or not*

Chapter Overview

In this chapter you will read about—

☐ **developing an assessment plan that includes a variety of assessment tools;**

☐ **establishing an environment conducive to successful performance;**

☐ **providing equal assessment opportunities for all students;**

☐ **managing time for assessment;**

☐ **conducting observations and interviews;**

☐ **promoting quality writing in mathematics;**

☐ **incorporating revisions of student work;**

☐ **promoting self- and peer-assessment;**

☐ **giving and reviewing homework;**

☐ **collecting evidence through tests and portfolios.**

LISTEN TO...

■ *Listen to a high school teacher discuss her assessment plan in the video "Teacher Insights from the Case Study Ferris Wheel" in the* Assessment Library for Grades K–12 *developed by the WBGH Educational Foundation (1998) of Boston.*

Establishing an Environment for Success

READ ABOUT...

■ *Read more about establishing conditions for success in* Measuring What Counts: A Conceptual Guide for Mathematics Assessment *by the Mathematical Sciences Education Board (1993) and* Student-Centered Classroom Assessment *by Richard Stiggins (1994).*

SOMETHING TO THINK ABOUT
Students encounter many barriers to learning mathematics. Some have failed often in the past. Some believe that mathematics is not relevant to them. Some have found that it is not popular to be good in mathematics. What strategies do you use to address these barriers? What do you do with students who come to your class with poor attitudes toward mathematics?

HOW CAN I ESTABLISH AN ENVIRONMENT THAT PROMOTES SUCCESSFUL PERFORMANCE ON ASSESSMENTS?

When we make decisions about assessing students, it is important to consider the classroom environment in which the students will work. Decisions about how we establish our learning environment for assessment will determine the kinds of evidence we obtain from students. Our assessment decisions also affect the quality of work our students provide us. Here is what some teachers think about in setting up their environment for successful performance.

TIPS FROM TEACHERS

■ *I always give my students some time in class to work on their homework. I let them work two or three carefully selected problems in groups to make sure they understand what they are supposed to do. Since I did this, my students complete assignments more often. Their questions the next day tend to focus on understanding rather than directions.*

■ *My students do a lot of group work in class, so it's only fair that my assessments include group work. I try to assess my students in groups. I also assess them individually quite often. Even when they work in groups, I occasionally assess them individually. It's important that I know how they work both in groups and individually.*

■ *Some of my students need more time to think through tasks. I have found that some of my students' work improved dramatically when I did not set time constraints.*

■ *I always try to have the right materials available during assessment. I try to be consistent in providing students the same materials for assessment that they use regularly in class. I make sure they have rulers, calculators, compasses, or other tools that they might need. These tools are always available and my students have to decide when it is appropriate to use them.*

■ *I try to set high expectations for my students and communicate those expectations in different ways. I share my goals and assessment system with my students at the beginning of the year. I involve them in assessment decisions. I have them score one another's work regularly. I never shy away from assigning them challenging tasks. My feedback to them is always positive and constructive.*

■ *I find out how my students feel about mathematics at the beginning of the year. I find out who loves it, who hates it, and who is neutral about it. I also find out why they feel as they do. This early assessment lets me know which students I should really concentrate on during the year.*

CHAPTER 3

Providing Equitable Opportunities

HOW CAN I ENSURE THAT ALL MY STUDENTS HAVE EQUITABLE OPPORTUNITIES TO SUCCEED WITH MY ASSESSMENTS?

As teachers, it is important that we be aware of how the nature of our assessments may affect student performance. Some students may be at a disadvantage even before the assessment starts.

Listed below are some questions to consider as you find, modify, or develop tasks that are accessible to all students:

- Do the tasks include wording or terminology familiar to students?

- Do they employ situations familiar to students regardless of cultural or socioeconomic background or gender?

- Do they make sense to all students?

- Do they motivate students by being relevant to them?

- Do they include helpful diagrams or pictures that clarify or invite students?

- Do they require information not available to all students?

Below is a task that may be inaccessible to some students.

> **Mr. Lopez invests $100 in a bank each year for 30 years. At an annual yield of 25% per year, how much will be in the bank at the end of the 30 years?**

This task can cause difficulties for the following reasons:

- Some students may not have had experiences with banks.

- Some students may not be motivated because Mr. Lopez's savings has little relevance to them.

- Some students may not have access to computers or calculators to work the problem.

- The interest rates and yield are unrealistic.

The task might be improved by having students open an account at a local bank, having students establish their own "class bank," or by making sure all students have access to, and can use, appropriate technology. Below is advice from teachers who have had success in removing barriers for their students.

READ ABOUT...

- *Read more about ensuring assessment accessibility in "Developing Communication Skills in Mathematics for Students with Limited English Proficiency" by Gilbert Cuevas (1991), "Making Mathematics Accessible to Latino Students: Rethinking Instructional Practice" by Lena Khisty (1997), and "Assessment and Equity" by Terri Belcher et al. (1997).*

TIPS FROM TEACHERS

- *I always read through a task before I give it to my students. If it's unfair, I revise it.*

- *I try to discuss terms that might be unfamiliar to my students.*

- *I often reword a task to make it easier to read.*

- *I ask students if they are familiar with the situation presented in the task.*

- *I make sure my students understand the task. If not, I clarify it by asking questions that point them in the right direction without giving away the solution strategies.*

- *I ask students to restate the task in their own words.*

Managing Time

READ ABOUT...

■ *Read about a group of high school teachers in a mathematics department struggling with the issue of finding time for portfolio assessment in "I Just Collected 120 Portfolios—Now What?" in* Mathematics Assessment: Cases and Discussion Questions for Grades 6–12 *(Bush 1999).*

■ *Read about two teachers who struggle with time constraints in trying new assessment approaches in "Tessellation Presentation" and "Does It Measure Up?" in* Mathematics Assessment: Cases and Discussion Questions for Grades 6–12 *(Bush 1999).*

HOW CAN I BEST MANAGE MY TIME FOR ASSESSMENT?

Finding time to assess with a variety of tools is often a problem, especially when tools like writing and projects are used. How do we find the time to assess in a variety of ways without sacrificing mathematics content? Time for these assessment strategies often competes with our need to cover the curriculum.

The variety of evidence we gather and the knowledge students gain through quality assessment is so valuable that finding time should be an important goal.

The best sources for tips about saving time are teachers who have implemented successful assessment plans. Here are some of their strategies for making more effective use of valuable time.

Tips for Saving Time

■ *I randomly select sample tasks to grade. I never grade all of them at once. For example, I may select two out of five assigned tasks to grade. I alert students beforehand about this practice and encourage them to make an attempt on all tasks.*

■ *I have students select their best items, such as their best homework assignment for the week or their best work on one homework assignment. I do this randomly so students will not just concentrate on one or two problems.*

■ *When scoring student work, I use only three levels—Finished Product, Ready for Revision, More Instruction Needed. The work scored "Ready for Revision" means that the mathematics is generally correct but the ideas could be communicated better. "More Instruction Needed" means that the student has developed misconceptions, has pursued a wrong strategy, or has made significant errors.*

■ *I use checklists for lengthy assessment assignments. I list all the task requirements on separate sheets and distribute them with the task. I ask students to check off the requirements as they work on the task. I review their checklists periodically.*

■ *I use a variety of assessments over a period of time. I use one tool or strategy at a time and wait until students reach a reasonable level of comfort with it before moving on to another tool or strategy.*

Managing Time

More Tips for Saving Time

■ *I list the most common errors or omissions on one sheet and distribute copies to my students. I have them check off the ones that apply to their work. Students use the sheet to correct their own work. This strategy is particularly helpful when I use the same task over a period of years.*

■ *I use group work a lot and often have students turn in work individually. Once or twice a month, however, I have students work in groups and submit their work as a group. This often reduces my grading threefold or fourfold.*

■ *I try to get my students comfortable with assessing one another and themselves. We establish scoring criteria together and sometimes score work together. In the beginning, I provide samples of excellent and poor student work to practice scoring so that students get some idea of what I mean by excellent work. We also work on ways to give constructive criticism to one another.*

■ *I give open-ended tasks to only one class at a time so that I will not be overwhelmed by grading a lot of them. This strategy works best when I can develop several versions of the same task.*

Conducting Observations

HOW CAN I MORE EFFECTIVELY OBSERVE STUDENTS AT WORK?

Observing students while they do mathematics in class gives us different information and a deeper understanding of our students' abilities. It allows us to watch the strategies students use to get answers. We have found observations that focus on specific student performance, rather than on all student performance at once, to be very practical and useful. Choosing the focus depends on what we want to learn about our students.

Observing whole classes can be overwhelming. Consider the following tips from experienced teachers to get started.

TIPS FROM TEACHERS

■ *I begin slowly, by observing one or two students for a few minutes each. During that time I record everything I observe. This helps me begin to develop an eye for observations.*

■ *I pick one or two students who are struggling and observe them as they engage in problem solving. I never intervene, and I tell them to try to ignore me.*

■ *I use a generic observation guide to assist me. I insert the categories that I value.*

Conducting Observations

SEE...

■ *See more samples of observation notes and checklists in* **figures 2.19** *and* **2.20** *in chapter 2.*

We offer an example of a checklist that can help us record and focus our observations. In **figure** 3.2 is a copy of an observation guide used by a teacher to monitor students' problem-solving strategies.

FIG. 3.2

OBSERVATION FORM

	Understands problem and selects strategy				Implements strategy accurately				Uses correct math language and notation to explain						
	Novice (1)	Apprentice (2)	Proficient (3)	Distinguished (4)	Novice (1)	Apprentice (2)	Proficient (3)	Distinguished (4)	Novice (1)	Apprentice (2)	Proficient (3)	Distinguished (4)	Novice (1)	Apprentice (2)	Proficir
Wendy		√12 /LEq				√12 /LEq				√12 /LEq					
John		√12				√12				√12					
Mark		√12 CB			√MS	√12 CB			√MS	√12 CB					
Chris	√CH /12				√CH /12				√CH /12						
Bobby		√12 /MS			√MS /12				√MS /12						
Ted		√12				√12			√12						
Gabe															
Tonya		√12 /LEq				√12 /LEq			/LEq	√12					
Shekia		√CH				√CH			√CH						
Mary		√12			√12				√12						
Karl		√12				√12				√12					
Anne		√VG /12				√VG /12				√VG /12					

Example of master-rubric chart, which was used to record observations.
The letters and numbers next to the check marks refer to different tasks.

From Vincent and Wilson (1996)

CHAPTER 3

Conducting Observations

Some teachers prefer to take notes about their observations. In **figure** 3.3 is a set of notes taken by a teacher observing her students work in groups. The teacher decided to focus her observations on students' mathematical thinking.

FIG. 3.3

TEACHER NOTES

READ ABOUT...

■ *For more about conducting observations, read* Assessment Alternatives in Mathematics *by David Clarke (1988), "Valuing What We See" by Doug Clarke and Linda Wilson (1994), and "Informal Assessment: A Story from the Classroom" by Mary Lynn Vincent and Linda Wilson (1996).*

Special Right Triangles
Group Work

Group 1	Group 2
Shane: Kept group on task ; Part 1 - noticed one leg is length of other leg multiplied by √3. **Jessie:** Kind of quiet, but involved ; Part 1 - noticed hypotenuse was length of one leg multiplied by 2 **Rosa:** Worked kind of independently but checked work with rest of group. **Coco:** Very vocal; not always sure about her responsibility to the group.	**Sana:** Tried to get discussion from others **Gina:** Checked answers with Sana **Jermaine:** Part 1 - discovered ratio of one leg to hypotenuse is 1 to 2; Sana; Gina helped in this discovery.
Group 3	**Group 4**
Hollis: Worked well with Michelle. **Michelle:** Tried to find explanations about relationships in text book. **Michael:** Somewhat quiet <u>NOTE</u>: This group did not finish - needed a member in group that was a good leader & mathematician.	**Heather:** Recognized all △'s on Part 1 were 30-60-90 **Meghan:** Together, Heather : Meghan discovered that one side of △ was equal to the other side multiplied by √3. - Part 1. **Nathan:** Nice job of keeping group on task - always trying to figure things out - good problem solver.
Group 5	**Group 6**
Kathryn: Worked alone but checked answers with Josh and Barrett. **Tory:** Somewhat disengaged ; Part 2 - recognized that all of the △'s were 45-45-90 **Josh:** ⎫ Worked well together - good problem **Barrett:** ⎭ solvers - recognized relationships between lengths of sides in Part 1 : Part 2	**Charlie:** ⎫ Discovered Ratio of leg to hypotenuse on Part 1 was 1 to 2. **Fritz:** ⎭ worked well together ; Part 2: Recognized length of leg times √2 gave length of hypotenuse. **Monique:** ⎫ Part: Discovered length of leg **Meredith:** ⎭ worked well together ; times √2 gave length of hypotenuse <u>NOTE</u>: This group had 2 groups within a group.
Group 7	
Greg: Asked good questions of others in group **Amanda:** Worked well with others; explained things to group members; recognized △'s were similar by AA; explained	**Matt:** Encouraged group to use Pythagorean Theorem to solve problems ; often sought my help instead of classmates' help. **Sandy:** Talked a lot, not always on task. to another student how to solve equation with √ in it.

Conducting Interviews

HOW CAN I MORE EFFECTIVELY INTERVIEW STUDENTS?

Interviews provide an excellent way to assess student thinking. Interviews may be spontaneous, to explore a student's confusion, or they may be planned and conducted regularly. The evidence we gather from student interviews gives us insight into students' understanding and thinking that might otherwise be missed in observations or examination of work. Interviews are excellent tools for uncovering students' mathematical misconceptions because they help us track the origins of their misconceptions.

Figure 3.4 illustrates how a teacher probes students' difficulties with graphing a rate problem. Note the kinds of questions asked by the teacher to reveal how the students are thinking.

FIG. 3.4

STUDENT INTERVIEW

Ships in the Fog

"Ugh. I just can't get this stuff."

"What's the matter, Billy?" Jill Jacobs asked as she walked toward the frustrated student.

"I can't even get the axes right," Billy Corbin replied shaking his head in disgust.

"Wait a minute, Billy. Just relax now. What exactly do you mean when you say that you 'can't get the axes right?'"

"I mean I keep running out of space."

"Okay, but now tell me exactly what you've been trying to do," Jill said in a soft tone intended to have a calming effect.

Billy exhaled a deep sigh and said, "One ship keeps going 3mm. this way (motioning left) every minute and the other keeps going this way (drawing his hand upward along the paper) 4 mm. every minute. I can't find something to use for both. If I let every space be 1, I don't have enough room to even show where the ships are when they begin...I mean, I'd need 900 spaces for crying out loud!"

Jill was surprised at what she was hearing. Until recently Billy had been a solid honor roll student, fairly astute and hardworking. Lately, however, his grades had slipped, due, Jill thought, to too many hours spent working at his after school job at a local pizzeria. Nevertheless, Jill never expected that what she perceived to be a simple task like scaling axes would cause him such trouble.

"Okay, Bill, let's slow down a bit. Why don't we reread the investigation together. Maybe it'll help us to frame the problem better in our minds."

Jill took her copy of the activity that she had taken from the Pacesetter Mathematics program (developed by the College Entrance Examination Board and Educational Testing Service) and began to read aloud:

Ships in the Fog*

Two ships are sailing in the fog and are being monitored by tracking equipment. As they come onto the observer's screen, one, the Andy Daria (AD), is at a point 900 mm. from the bottom left screen along the lower edge. The other one, the Helsinki (H), is located at a point 100 mm. above the lower left corner along the left edge. One minute later the positions have changed. The AD has moved to a location on the screen that is 3 mm. "west" and 2 mm. "north" of its previous location. The H has moved 4 mm. "east" and 1 mm. "north". Assume that they will continue to move at a constant speed on their respective linear courses.

Will the two ships collide if they maintain their speeds and directions? If so, when? If not, how close do they actually come to each other?

"Okay, do you really understand the situation and what the problem is asking?"

*Pacesetter Mathematics (1994). Pre-calculus through modeling. New York: The College Board, Educational Testing Service.

CHAPTER 3

Conducting Interviews

FIG. 3.4 (Continued)

STUDENT INTERVIEW

"Yeah, I get it okay. I did before. I just can't figure out how to do it," Billy blurted out with obvious exasperation.

"Well," Jill continued, "do you need to have the spaces along one axis represent the same distance as the spaces along the other axis? What do you think, Phong?"

Phong—A Different Point of View

Jill directed her question to Billy's partner, Phong Chantapho, a girl whose family moved to the United States from Laos when Phong was only a year old. Phong spoke fluent English and did well at mathematics. She was also shy, often needing encouragement to speak up.

"No." replied Phong, "but it's easier if you do."

"Why?" queried Jill.

"Because when you look at how the ships move, the y distance to x distance looks real. If the x and y's were different, it wouldn't look like real life and it'd be harder to understand."

"So, you're saying, Phong, that if the x and y scales are identical, then the ratio of the ships' vertical distance covered to that of the horizontal distance moved is the same as that ratio in real life, so the path direction, or bearing, is the same as in real life? Did I understand you accurately?"

"Yes," said Phong in a tone barely above a whisper. Jill wondered if Phong really did understand what she had just said. In fact, the situation seemed a little complicated, even to Jill.

"For now, you might as well use equal distances along each axis as you've always done. But let's get back to the problem of running out of space. Have you considered using another unit of time, rather than a minute, that'd make the units of distance larger so that you wouldn't need as many spaces along each axis?" Jill continued.

"Hours," Phong replied immediately.

"Why hours?"

"Because the ships go farther in one hour than they do in one minute."

"Good, Phong. Could you explain this to Billy and me by referring to the horizontal or x motion of the Andy Daria?"

"I think so. The ship moves 3 mm. left in one minute. That means it'd move 60 times 3 or 180 mm. left in one hour."

"Sounds good to me," supported Jill. "What would the y motion be like?"

"Instead of going 2 mm. up, it'd go 120 mm. up in an hour."

"Excellent, Phong. Billy, how much would the Helsinki move in each direction in one hour? Remember, it moves 4 mm. right and 1 mm. up in one minute."

"Then it'd go 60 times that. Let me see...that'd be 240 mm. right and 60 mm. up. Right?"

From Merseth and Karp (in press)

From beginning to end Jill, the teacher, probed for understanding. When students responded, she probed for justification of their answers. After the interview, Jill wrote the following notes:

"Phong has a strong grasp of graphing and can think proportionally. She used good reasoning in solving the problem."

"Billy understands the problem but cannot easily translate to a graph. He needs help in moving from words to graphs."

Interviews can be very time-consuming, especially in large classes. To the right are comments from teachers who have found ways to interview their students regularly.

TIPS FROM TEACHERS

■ *I conduct interviews when the rest of the class is working on seat assignments or group work.*

■ *I do interviews with students over the course of the whole grading period so that I can individually interview each student at least once.*

■ *I conduct my interviews with students in small groups so that other students can participate in the discussion. It also cuts down on the number of interviews I conduct.*

Conducting Interviews

READ ABOUT...

■ *Read more about interviewing students in* Myths, Models, Good Questions, and Practical Suggestions *edited by Jean Stenmark (1991).*

Interview questions should be nonjudgmental and designed to detect students' thinking. Below are some generic questions we might ask students about solving problems.

■ When you began to solve the problem, what were you thinking?

■ Why did you choose to solve the problem that way?

■ Can you show your solution in another form?

■ How would the answer be affected if the numbers were bigger or you did not have a certain piece of information?

■ What was it about the numbers that led you to reason this way about them?

■ How did you know to...?

■ Does it make a difference that...?

■ Is one of these answers better or are they equally good?

These questions serve our instructional purposes. When we record and compile student responses, they serve our assessment purposes.

Promoting Higher-Quality Writing

TIPS FROM TEACHERS

■ *I try to improve my students' writing about mathematics by breaking down the writing process into several components and teaching it through a step-by-step process. I write comments on their work and have them work in groups to revise it.*

■ *I have students write to a variety of audiences—a younger child, a best friend, the principal, a parent, or the president of a company.*

■ *I offer written comments on students' first drafts or have other students give suggestions about how to clarify the writing.*

■ *I ask English teachers how they help students improve their writing. Then I reinforce that approach in my classes.*

HOW CAN I PROMOTE HIGHER-QUALITY WRITING FROM MY STUDENTS?

Students become better writers and thinkers of mathematics when they have regular opportunities to write about mathematics. Many high school mathematics teachers have begun to require student writing in their classes. To the left are some suggestions from these teachers.

Here is an example of writing instructions that promote communicating about mathematical thinking (from *They're Counting on Us*, California Mathematics Council [1995]):

Your first writing assignment has two parts. First, you are to restate the problem in your own words. Then you are to show all of your work, as well as your final answer. Be sure to—

1. write your solution as if the reader knows nothing about the problem;

2. show all of your math work, including all calculations;

3. organize your work into either a step-by-step plan and solution or some kind of chart or table that is easy to read and follow;

4. proofread your work so that you are sure you have not left out any important words or calculations;

5. make sure this is your best work and that it is neat and legible.

CHAPTER 3

Promoting Higher-Quality Writing

Diane Miller (1991, p. 520) offers the following helpful tips for writing in mathematics classes:

- Decide how long to let students write, and set a timer.

- When preparing a lesson plan, include writing questions that relate to the lesson.

- Ask students to write to a friend, family member, or neighbor.

- Have students write at the beginning of class to help them make the transition from previous activities or lessons.

- Have students write at the end of class to assess their understanding or impressions of how class went.

- Join the students in writing.

- Do not offer extrinsic rewards such as points for writing. Share the intrinsic benefits of writing.

- Do not penalize students when they do not write.

- Be patient.

Figure 3.5 provides a sample of good writing from a high school student. Note how he used tables and graphs to communicate his ideas. Also note how clearly he explains his thinking.

FIG. 3.5

SOMETHING TO THINK ABOUT
What are the advantages and disadvantages of *not* offering intrinsic rewards, like points and grades, to encourage students to write in mathematics classes?

READ ABOUT...

- *Read more about writing in mathematics classrooms in "Writing to Learn Mathematics" and "Begin Mathematics Class with Writing" by Diane Miller (1991, 1992), "Assessing Students' Thinking through Writing" by Jennifer Mayer and Susan Hillman (1996),* Writing to Learn Mathematics *by Joan Countryman (1992),* Writing to Learn Mathematics and Science *by Paul Connolly and Teresa Vilardi (1989), and "Connecting Writing to the Mathematics Curriculum" by David Pugalee (1997).*

SAMPLE OF GOOD WRITING

M and M Break

My group took a large bag of M and M's and poured them flatly on the table. We then spread them out so that a M was or was not showing. The M and M's with the M showing were removed from the M and M's without the M showing. We then gave the M and M's with the M showing to the class and started the process over with the others. This process was repeated until we ran out of M and M's. This T-chart represents our process and and answers.

Trial Number	Number of Candies Left
0	522
1	268
2	142
3	72
4	40
5	25
6	17
7	11
8	9
9	0

We discovered that the number of candies left depended on the trial number. This means that the number of candies is the dependent variable and the trial number is the independent variable.

Using a graphing calculator, we substituted in the known points to form a graph. from this graph we were able to determine to use the equation $A = Ce^{kt}$.

Promoting Higher-Quality Writing

FIG. 3.5 (Continued)

SAMPLE OF GOOD WRITING

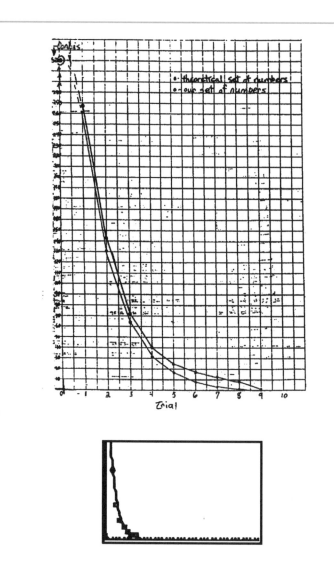

We found that C represents the initial amount by substituting 0 into the equation $A = Ce^{kt}$. This is true because if you substitute 0 for t, C must equal 522 for A to equal 522. This means that C has to be the initial amount, which equals 522.

To find what takes place of e we expected around .5 or half, because of probability.

We tested .55 and it produced a graph that passed through our known points. So, our equation is $y = 522(.55^k)$.

In theory, half of the M and M's should remain after each shake. Our data doesn't exactly match the theoretical set of numbers, because anything could happen. If we had been given a larger set of original data we would have been closer to the theoretical set of numbers.

Revising Student Work

HOW MUCH REVISION OF STUDENT WORK SHOULD I ALLOW?

Guiding students in revising their work provides clarification of our expectations and can help students further reflect on their work and the work of their peers. It communicates to students that good work requires time and revision.

Although getting students to revise their work can be time-consuming, most teachers who do it believe the time is well spent. To the right is how some teachers address time constraints in guiding student revisions.

From these tips, it should be clear that all the work of revising need not fall on us. After initially showing students how to correct their papers, we can gradually give them more responsibility.

The number of revisions we allow students is our decision. Some believe students should revise as many times as they like. Others believe that students should revise once. As students gain experience with the revision process, their work will usually require fewer revisions.

WHAT QUESTIONS SHOULD I ASK IN REVISING STUDENT WORK?

Some key questions we might ask students while talking about their revisions include—

- What was the task asking?

- What would a clear explanation include?

- Would someone not in our class who picked up your paper understand your answers and how you got them?

- Are all the elements of the answer included?

- How can this response be more precise? More concise? Clearer? More convincing?

TIPS FROM TEACHERS

■ *I quickly read over the students' papers and make no marks or comments. I keep a running list of faults and problems. I take the papers back to class and share the faults and problems I found with my students. I give them their papers back and ask them to revise and resubmit in two days.*

■ *I set aside a block of time in class for peer review. (I learned this from colleagues in history and English.) I make sure students have a clear understanding of my expectations and a set of questions to ask about each paper. I have students exchange papers. I give them time to read and write comments. I also allow time for oral feedback. Students then get their papers back and revise them.*

■ *I use sticky notes to write comments on my students' work. I hand back the papers for revision. The sticky notes are temporary and allow for minor revisions.*

■ *I select papers that show a range of response levels. I type the answers or cover up the names to make the responses anonymous. I ask students to score the papers using criteria that I developed. Then we discuss how to make the papers better.*

Revising Student Work

WHAT KINDS OF FEEDBACK SHOULD I GIVE DURING REVISIONS?

Giving constructive feedback without giving answers is often difficult. Usually the best strategy is to keep comments general rather than specific. Note the comments made by a teacher on the student work in **figure 3.6**. She used questions to encourage the student to clarify her thinking and writing.

FIG. 3.6

STUDENT WORK WITH TEACHER COMMENTS

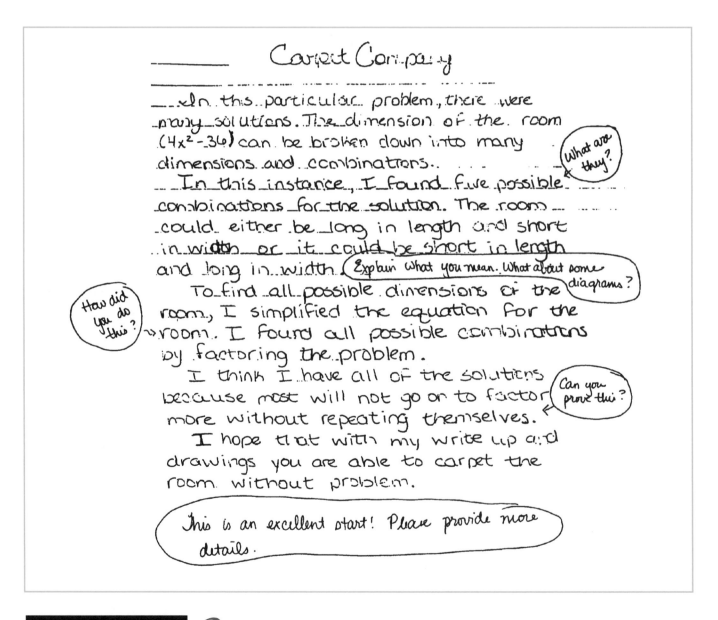

Carpet Company

In this particular problem, there were many solutions. The dimension of the room $(4x^2 - 36)$ can be broken down into many dimensions and combinations.

What are they?

In this instance, I found five possible combinations for the solution. The room could either be long in length and short in width or it could be short in length and long in width.

Explain what you mean. What about some diagrams?

How did you do this?

To find all possible dimensions of the room, I simplified the equation for the room. I found all possible combinations by factoring the problem.

I think I have all of the solutions because most will not go on to factor more without repeating themselves.

Can you prove this?

I hope that with my write up and drawings you are able to carpet the room without problem.

This is an excellent start! Please provide more details.

CHAPTER 3

Promoting Student Self-Assessment

HOW CAN I BETTER PROMOTE STUDENT SELF-ASSESSMENT?

If students reflect on their work and their thought processes, they often discover for themselves both strengths and areas that need improvement. As with other assessments, the tools we use to promote reflection and self-assessment are varied. When students are first asked to reflect or assess their own work, many of their responses appear superficial. At this time it is helpful to furnish them with clear expectations and guidelines. **Figure 3.7** provides an example of a checklist that a teacher used to help students assess their work.

FIG. 3.7

GUIDE FOR COMPLETING PROBLEM OF THE WEEK

Guide to Completing the Problem of the Week

Your solution will be graded on the basis of the strength you show in each of the four critical thinking skills listed below as well as on the overall quality of presentation. Use the following checklist to guide you in writing your solution.

1. Conceptual understanding of the problem

❑ I used diagrams, pictures, graphs, and symbols to explain my work.

❑ I used all the important information.

❑ I have thought about the problem carefully and feel as if I know what I'm talking about.

2. Procedural knowledge

❑ I used appropriate mathematical computations, terms, and formulas.

❑ I used mathematical ideas and language precisely.

❑ I checked my answer for reasonableness.

3. Problem-solving skills and strategies

❑ I looked for other possible ways to solve the problem.

❑ I used problem-solving strategies that show good reasoning.

❑ My work is clear and organized.

4. Communication

❑ I communicated clearly and effectively to the reader.

❑ In my solution, one step seems to flow to the next.

❑ I used mathematics vocabulary and terminology clearly.

❑ I have justified my strategy and reasonableness of my solution clearly.

❑ I have proofread my solution for clarity of presentation.

5. Overall quality of presentation

❑ The overall apearance of my work is attractive, clear, and easy for the reader to read.

❑ Diagrams are drawn neatly, clearly, and accurately; axes are labeled properly and clearly.

❑ Equations are written neatly, using a consistent format and style.

Promoting Student Self-Assessment

The record sheet in **figure 3.8** was designed by a precalculus teacher to have students assess themselves and keep records of their progress.

FIG. 3.8

PRECALCULUS RECORD SHEET

PRECALCULUS RECORD SHEET

NAME _____   2ND QUARTER SHEET (93-94)

HOMEWORK

	TIME SPENT	QUALITY CHECK (+,√,-)	UNDER-STANDING (U,NY)		TIME SPENT	QUALITY CHECK (+,√,-)	UNDER-STANDING (U,NY)
#1				#13			
#2				#14			
#3				#15			
#4				#16			
#5				#17			
#6				#18			
#7				#19			
#8				#20			
#9				#21			
#10				#22			
#11				#23			
#12				#24			

PROBLEM SOLVING ACTIVITIES (+,√,IP, NY)

#1-Project Problem   1ST DRAFT [ ] 2ND DRAFT [ ] 3RD DRAFT [ ]

#2-Project History Section   1ST DRAFT [ ] 2ND DRAFT [ ] 3RD DRAFT [ ]

#3 -   1ST DRAFT [ ] 2ND DRAFT [ ] 3RD DRAFT [ ]

#4 -   1ST DRAFT [ ] 2ND DRAFT [ ] 3RD DRAFT [ ]

CONCEPTS-WRITE IN ACTIVITIES THAT DEMONSTRATE YOUR UNDERSTANDING

#1 Find roots of various functions using appropriate methods and determine their significance

#2 Describe the behavior of various functions (max/min, continuity, asymptotes, turning points, variable slope, symmetry)

#3 Identify and use transformation of functions

#4 Apply rate of change to various functions

#5 Use matrices to solve problems

Promoting Student Self-Assessment

Some teachers ask students to write journals. Providing students with clear criteria for writing in their journals will help them understand what we expect from them. Consider the following guidelines for students.

Please communicate freely and openly in your journal. Your teacher will review your journal periodically, looking for evidence of the following:

- Communication (verbal and pictorial) of your mathematical thinking (you try to make clear and detailed explanations and diagrams)

- Mathematical reasoning

- Personally derived solutions to math problems

- Creative insights or deep thinking (e.g., you make conjectures and generalizations, etc.)

- Monitoring and reporting your feelings (disequilibrium, AHA!, joy, frustration, etc., that you experienced while working on a problem or during a class activity)

- Awareness of your own mathematical growth, strengths, and needs

It is important *not* to erase a journal entry, even if you feel that what you wrote is wrong. Instead, show growth by adding new ideas (write the date that you make the addition), or on another page describe how your thinking has changed.

READ ABOUT...

■ *Read about a teacher who uses self-assessment in her geometry class in "Peer and Self-Assessment" in* Mathematics Assessment: Cases and Discussion Questions for Grades 6–12 *(Bush 1999).*

■ *For more information about promoting reflection, read* Mathematics Assessment: Myths, Models, Good Questions, and Practical Suggestions *edited by Jean Stenmark (1991) and "Student Self-Assessment in Mathematics" by Patricia Kenney and Edward Silver (1993).*

■ *Read about a teacher who is concerned about students' scoring their work and the work of others in "A Difference of Opinion" in* Mathematics Assessment: Cases and Discussion Questions for Grades 6–12 *(Bush 1999).*

Promoting Peer Assessment

HOW CAN I BETTER PROMOTE PEER ASSESSMENT?

In addition to self-assessment, we may also use peer assessment. We may ask students to score one another's work and justify the scores. It is sometimes interesting to compare the self-scores and justifications with those given by other students.

In **figures 3.9** and **3.10** are examples of how two pairs of high school stu-

FIG. 3.9

STUDENT WORK—PEER ASSESSMENT #1

Peer Review of Data Project   Reviewers _____

Names of students whose paper is being reviewed _____ _____

Pretend you are a student who is taking precalculus at another school. Read the paper to see if you understand the ideas. Do the writer's explain what they are doing and why? A list of the major components of the paper follow. Use this list to make notes on suggestions for those parts of the paper.

1. Introduction, what is this data all about? Sources cited?

    *Where did data come from?
    Labor Force vs Time
    Explain what data is about.

2. Explanation of how they search for and find a good model.

    good show of trial and error

3. Support for finding the model. Are the math steps shown? Are there graphs? What about residuals? What about error bounds? got all

    show math steps for the aspects you found
    graphs, residuals, error bounds?

4. Discussion of limitations and capabilities of the model.

    domain and range limitations
    extrapolation and interpolation
        how relevant to real world

5. Writing/organization of paper.

    very good
        data analysis, neat graphs, combining
        graphs and typing

6. General comments.

    more background
        step by step
        over all good

dents scored other students' work. Note how the teacher lists the criteria students are to use. The students not only judge the work but also offer rationales for their judgments.

FIG. 3.10

STUDENT WORK—PEER ASSESSMENT #2

Peer Review of Data Project   Reviewers

Names of students whose paper is being reviewed _____

Pretend you are a student who is taking precalculus at another school. Read the paper to see if you understand the ideas. Do the writer's explain what they are doing and why? A list of the major components of the paper follow. Use this list to make notes on suggestions for those parts of the paper.

1. Introduction, what is this data all about? Sources cited?

Synthetic chemicals, alligators per km and years. Sources are not sited but an article is included for reference. Good background.

2. Explanation of how they search for and find a good model.

they took semi log and log-log and compared the two maybe a little more about subtracting 1.5 from y-data.

3. Support for finding the model. Are the math steps shown? Are there graphs? What about residuals? What about error bounds?

Math steps are shown. There are graphs. Residuals are included. THERE ARE NO ERROR BOUNDS. Graphs are pretty. Though.

4. Discussion of limitations and capabilities of the model.

No interpolation or extrapolation of data. Little post-data analysis + discussion. Let's work on additional discussion to include maybe seperate conclusion section

5. Writing/organization of paper.

Color is very nice   Organized well
Graphs are pretty   It makes me happy.
"homemade"

6. General comments.

Extremely warm, friendly, easy to understand
Perhaps More post-data analyses!
Units need a little work   maybe incorporate bit
                            HIGHLIGHT ARTICLE
                            graph of Article in report

Promoting Peer Assessment

FIGURE 3.11

POW ASSESSMENT

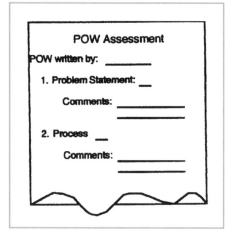

FIGURE 3.12

POW PEER ASSESSMENT

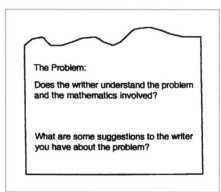

Below is a vignette about a teacher who gravitated toward peer assessment and student self-assessment to save time.

Evaluating extended problems has caused headaches for me. Students put a lot of time into write-ups and solving problems. It is important to me that I get them involved in the assessment, give them usable feedback, and spend a reasonable amount of time grading the write-ups. The first year of assessing extended problems, Problems of the Week, I wanted to give careful feedback on each section of the write-up. I thought this would help students understand my expectations for a good write-up.

*I filled out the POW Assessment form in **figure 3.11** for every student and attached it to the student work. This was very time-consuming. Also, students were confused about my comments. I was also concerned about the amount of paper used to provide feedback. The next year, I moved to Post-it notes. I was able to pinpoint my comments to a sentence, calculation, or diagram. This still proved to be very time-consuming. By the end of the year, I was concerned about student understanding and involvement in the process. As a result, I designed the Problem of the Week Peer Assessment in **figure 3.12**. It got students involved in looking at pieces of work critically. I hoped it would decrease the amount of time I spent looking at write-ups. Students found it difficult to be honest and constructive. Some revisions took place. The time I spent grading was about the same. The latest step in my journey to assess extended problems involved the students in self-assessment. I developed a specific rubric (see **fig. 3.13**) for such problems. (See chapter 4 for a discussion about rubrics.) Each student determined the level of his or her write-up and answered a few questions. I changed to this form because I found that I was making similar comments on many papers. I designed the rubric to capture those comments. This saved time. I still make individual comments on Post-it's, and students review their assessments and mine. I was also able to see how they viewed their work and to communicate my expectations. I am still working on my assessment.*

Promoting Peer Assessment

FIG. 3.13

POW SELF-ASSESSMENT

POW #11 Rubric

IP Your write-up is at this level if it exhibits one or more of the following:

▢ All parts of the write-up are not present or not complete.

▢ Your rule is not explained from the information in your process.

▢ Many patterns are found and explained. You use a combination of the patterns to find the chair to sit in but not for any chair.

√ Your write-up is at this level if it exhibits all of the following:

▢ All parts of the write-up are present.

▢ You determine the rule for which chair to sit in for any number of knights.

▢ You explain how you found your rule.

▢ Explanation is thorough enough so that no assumptions are made by the reader.

+ In addition to the requirements for a √ , you have done both of the following:

▢ You have found the rule using more than one method. These methods are independent of each other. You explain the relationship between the methods.

▢ The write-up contains elegant communication (clear diagrams, concise explanations, strong mathematical arguments, etc.)...

Student Assessment:

▢ Indicate what level your POW is at given the description.

▢ How much time did you spend on this? Was it sufficient for a quality effort?

▢ What math concepts or skills were developed?

Giving and Reviewing Homework

HOW DO I GIVE EFFECTIVE HOMEWORK?

Homework is an important part of learning and assessment. Students who do homework regularly usually find greater success in our courses. The mechanics of encouraging homework preparation through assessment activities, however, can be demanding and time-consuming.

Homework can serve many assessment purposes. It can inform us about our students'—

- ability to perform mathematical procedures;

- ability to apply concepts and skills to new situations;

- readiness for new concepts, ideas, or topics;

- readiness for other types of assessments.

Because of their potential as sources of assessment, homework tasks should be designed in accordance with the criteria outlined in chapter 2. The textbook series Contemporary Mathematics in Context by the Core-Plus Mathematics Project uses modeling, organizing, reflecting, and extending to present students with a variety of assessment tasks through homework assignments. **Figure 3.14** shows examples of some of these tasks.

CHAPTER *3*

Giving and Reviewing Homework

FIG. 3.14

HOMEWORK ASSIGNMENT

Modeling

1. Recall that data on population growth showed a U.S. population of 248 million in 1990 a growth rate of 0.7%, and 0.9 million immigrants annually. Use your calculator or computer software and this information to answer the following questions.

   a. When will the population reach 300 million?

   b. When will the population double?

Organizing

1. The studies of populations changing over time can be represented with graphs if you form ordered pairs of (*year, population*) data. Recall that the 1990 population of Brazil was 145 million people and that the growth rate each year is about 1.9%. Use your calculator to plot the (*year, population*) data for each ten-year period from 1990 to 2050.

   a. Make a sketch of the plot and write a brief description summarizing the pattern of the plotted data.

   Note: Sketches for parts b and c should be made on the same set of axes.

   b. Sketch the pattern of (*year, population*) data you would expect in Brazil if the birth rates increased.

   c. Sketch the pattern of (*year, population*) data you would expect in Brazil if the birth and death rates were equal.

   d. Explain how the pattern of points on each graph shows the *NOW* to *NEXT* change in the population.

Reflecting

3. In the population model of this lesson, you made estimations based on given assumptions about how the populations would change. Do you know anything about differences between Brazil and the United States that would help explain the differences in assumptions?

Extending

1. The kinds of models of change used in studying populations are sometimes quite different from the ones you have investigated so far. For example, many psychologists study the way people learn and remember information. Suppose that when school closes in June you know the meaning of 500 Spanish words, but you don't study or speak Spanish during the summer vacation.

   a. One model of memory suggests that during each week of the summer you will forget 5% of the words you know at the beginning of that week. Make a table showing the (*weeks, words remembered*) data pairs for 10 weeks and describe the pattern of data in the table.

   b. A second model suggests that you will forget 20 words each week. Make a table showing the (*weeks, words remembered*) data pairs for 10 weeks following this model and describe the pattern of data in that table.

   c. Graph the data from the two models and describe the patterns of data in those graphs.

   d. How would answers to parts a through c be different if you knew only 300 words at the start of summer?

From Coxford et al. (1998, pp. 116–20)

Giving and Reviewing Homework

HOW CAN I REVIEW HOMEWORK EFFECTIVELY?

Students will value homework if their thoughts and difficulties are addressed consistently and immediately. Going over homework, especially difficult assignments, can be time-consuming. The vignette below describes how one teacher makes going over homework a learning experience for her students.

"Hi, Sarah. Great soccer game yesterday." "That was an awesome game! But guys, we need to talk about that homework. I got several of the questions, but I could not do any of the problems on page 237. How did you do these?" "Let's see what I did. For some reason those questions made sense to me. Let me find my paper." All three students start going through notebooks to find homework so they can compare methods.

Mrs. Crane circulates around the room delivering yellow homework cards to each cluster (see fig. 3.15). The card includes the date, the name of each student in a group, the number of correct responses, and at the bottom the total possible. She announces to the class that today's assignment is worth 6 points—one for each homework problem. Students are busy talking to one another—comparing answers and looking at different ways each has done the problem. Members of each group decide the number of points each gets for this assignment and record their decisions on the yellow card. Mrs. Crane stops briefly to talk with each group to see what the students think of their work. The room is noisy, but it is clear the students are engaged—this is an important time.

Within the first ten minutes, Mrs. Crane has taken roll, talked with each group, assessed homework preparation, and has an idea of the problems that need more discussion. The students have shared ideas, assessed their work, and reviewed the work of others. Now they can take some time with problem 6, which has everyone perplexed!

By the way, this is November. In September, this activity took longer, since Mrs. Crane helped students understand the mechanics of this process. She helped students understand her expectations and made sure that members of each group worked together. Ten percent of a student's quarter grade is determined by his or her classroom performance, which includes this kind of daily homework assessment and work in groups. Students learn the value of self-assessment, the value of discussing techniques and methods, and the importance of being prepared. The best part is that they learn not only from Mrs. Crane but also from themselves and from their peers.

FIG. 3.15

HOMEWORK CARD

Name: \ Date	3/13	3/25	3/26	3/?	4/14	4/32	4/24	5/5	5/16	5/7										Total
Leslie M.	6	a	5	8	9	3	6	9	a	4		99								
Andrew G.	6	14	5	8	4	3	4	5	2	4		80								
Lyle M.	5	11	5	8	9	3	6	5	2	0		78								
Total	6	16	5	5	9	3	9	9	0	4										

Collecting Evidence through Tests

HOW CAN I COLLECT A VARIETY OF EVIDENCE THROUGH TESTS?

Even the most innovative assessors at the high school level continue to use tests in their assessment program. Some teachers use tests to comply with administrative mandates; others use them to meet goals of a balanced assessment program. Tests are likely to remain a significant part of classroom assessment, so modifying their design is often an excellent and comfortable first step toward changing our assessment practices.

In the eyes of students, what we test is what we value. Our response to the question "Will it be on the test?" carries a very strong message about the link between curriculum and assessment. It is important, therefore, that our tests measure what we value, not just what is easy to assess. Some of the abilities tests may assess are—

- thinking about mathematical ideas;

- making choices about strategies;

- making inferences;

- interpreting information;

- assessing one's own results;

- communicating mathematical ideas;

- justifying one's work.

The algebra 1 test (referred to by the teacher as a "Survey of Progress") in **figure 3.16** illustrates how one teacher chose to assess some of these abilities.

Note the variety in these tasks. In the first task, students read a graph and write a relationship. In the second task, students apply the concept of slope to a real situation. In the third task, students draw graphs based on relationships.

Collecting Evidence through Tests

READ ABOUT...

■ *Read how a teacher prepares her students for external tests in "An Assessment Experiment" in* Mathematics Assessment: Cases and Discussion Questions for Grades 6–12 *(Bush 1999).*

FIG. 3.16

SURVEY OF PROGRESS #3

SURVEY OF PROGRESS #3
(new nomenclature for a test)
Algebra 1
October 14, 1996

EACH answer is to be written using at least one complete English sentence with some explanation of how you arrived at your answer.

1. Hampton has a cold-water spring that is open to the public. The water continuously pours out of a pipe, and a person can fill a container with it. The graph at the right shows the rate at which the water is pouring out of the pipe. From the graph—

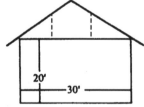

Water Flow at Exeter Spring

(a) estimate the number of minutes it would take to fill a 6-gallon container;

(b) estimate the number of gallons that comes out of the pipe in 30 seconds;

(c) express the rate at which the water comes out and label the rate;

(d) write a relationship between the number of gallons and the number of minutes, identifying the variables used.

2. The building code in Kensington states that no building can be more than 35 feet tall. A carpenter constructing the building pictured at the right would like to pitch the roof so that its vertical rise is 10 inches for each foot of horizontal distance.

(a) With the other dimensions as given, will she be able to do this? Explain.

(b) Two roof supports (indicated by dotted lines) are to be placed 6 feet from the center line of the building. Ignoring the thickness of the supports, how long must they be? Explain.

3. For each of the following situations, draw a simple graph showing the relationship between the time elapsed (horizontal axis) and the speed (vertical axis) of the object. Label the units on your axes. Use the graph paper provided.

(a) A car being put through a bumper test travels along at a constant speed until it crashes into the wall.

(b) You start a running workout by jogging and then running hard for a short time; you then jog and run hard again; finally you slow down and stop.

(c) A roller coaster begins by slowly climbing up a steep ramp and then zooms down the other side. (Plot the car's progress just to the bottom of the first hill.)

(d) A car speeds along the highway until an officer pulls it over and gives the occupant a ticket. The car then continues on at a more reasonable speed.

CHAPTER *3*

Collecting Evidence through Tests

Tests that include a variety of assessment tasks will require more thinking and effort from students. Therefore, it is important that we think about the way in which our tests are administered. Below is how one teacher now uses tests.

READ ABOUT...

■ *Read more about constructing tests in "Improving Classroom Tests as a Means of Improving Assessment" by Denisse Thompson, Charlene Beckmann, and Sharon Senk (1997) and "The Mathematics Test: A New Role for an Old Friend" by John Rahn Manon (1995).*

1. Students perform tasks on the test and hand in their work.

2. I indicate responses that are correct and those that are wrong. For wrong responses, I raise questions about students' methods.

3. I return tests to students for revision.

4. Students provide feedback to me as part of the homework assignment for the next day. Questions asked might be—

■ Were the problems fair?

■ Did you understand what I was asking for, what my expectations were?

■ Did the problems enable you to demonstrate what you had learned in this unit?

■ What did you learn about the topics, or yourself in completing the test?

■ Did you understand my feedback or commentary?

■ Do you agree with my commentary?

5. I collect revisions and student feedback or and determine a grade. The grade can be based heavily on their initial performance, but some credit is warranted for good thinking or rethinking in the revision process.

6. I provide students correct solutions, perhaps copied from exemplary student solutions.

Tests may come in many different formats. Not all tests need to be given within a class period with students working individually and under a time constraint. Some interesting variations might include group tests, student-designed tests, and take-home tests.

Group Tests

■ Write a test with problems that are more challenging than those found on a typical test. Then have students work on them in small groups.

■ Walk around while students work and take note of their conversations and strategies.

■ Require each group to submit solutions and written justifications.

Collecting Evidence through Tests

TAKE-HOME TESTS
Students who suffer great anxiety when taking a test in class often benefit greatly from this kind of test. They could use outside resources—perhaps not other people, but at least their notes, their texts, other texts, or the Web. Most important, the time constraint is removed—a huge factor for many students.

Student–Designed Tests

- Have students prioritize important concepts of the chapter or sections and select problems that address a fair distribution of topics.

- Make sure students write tasks that are clear to the reader, with unambiguous wording, and with sufficient information to solve the problem.

- Have students create a grading scale and solutions to the problems.

- After review and some revision by students and teacher working together, give the test to other small groups as an in-class test.

Read below how a teacher had her calculus students design their own test.

Last year in my calculus class I gave the following task for my final exam:

Think back on all the topics we've studied this semester and create (do not copy) five problems that are representative of these topics. Then solve the problems. Your problems should demonstrate the upper limit of your understanding of the concepts (so that I expect more complex problems from a student with a sophisticated understanding than from a student with just a basic grasp of concepts). Include a summary reflection (one page) on this process and also comment on what you have learned this semester.

Students had a week to do the assignment. The results were wonderful—students rose to the challenge well. Grading was based on how appropriate the difficulty was for their ability and understanding, how accurately they solved their own problems, and how representative the problems were. Students were amazed at how much they had learned, and they liked having some control over the questions. I definitely will adapt this, perhaps using it on a quarter basis in other classes and starting with younger students.

CHAPTER *3*

Collecting Evidence through Portfolios

A number of my colleagues had students complete portfolios this semester. All seemed to have some success with this form of assessment. Students were asked to turn in their portfolios about ten days before the semester's end to give time for grading and return of the portfolios before the exam study period began. For many students, the activity of designing their portfolios began the semester's work. If students understand your expectations, this is an activity that they can control. The decisions and assessment are theirs.

Early in the year I talk with my students about the portfolio, mainly to remind them to keep documents. During the semester, I try to identify good entries when they hand in a paper or do some activity. Near the end of the semester, I give specific instructions on how many documents they need, how to write on each, and when the portfolio is due. I ask each student to write about his or her work and progress during the semester. I offer lots of ideas for this: a letter to their favorite math teacher, a letter of advice for students next September, or an "If I Could Relive First Semester" paper. One of my colleagues asks students to write a summary of what they have learned. These additions are often the most thoughtful pieces in the portfolio.

This year I tried a new activity that vastly improved the portfolios. During the first quarter, each student did a sample entry as a graded assignment.

READ ABOUT...

■ *Read about a high school mathematics department's struggle with portfolios in "I Just Collected 120 Portfolios—Now What?" in* Mathematics Assessment: Cases and Discussion Questions for Grades 6–12 *(Bush 1999).*

There is no universal definition of a mathematics portfolio or of its purpose in assessing student learning. All portfolios have some common characteristics:

■ They represent collections of student work.

■ The collection represents work done over a substantial period of time—at least a two- or three-week unit.

■ The collection is useful to teachers and students as well as to parents and administrators.

Portfolios, however, may differ from one another with respect to the following characteristics:

Control—student selection vs. teacher selection

Self-Reflection—student evaluates vs. teacher evaluates

Quality—work represents growth over time vs. work includes best work

Evidence—work reflects math goals and habits of mind vs. work reflects math goals only

Portfolios can be an excellent means to collect a variety of pieces of student work. They are particularly beneficial as an overview of work over a quarter or a semester.

Collecting Evidence through Portfolios

READ ABOUT...

■ *Read more about portfolio assessment in "Student Mathematics Portfolio: More than a Display Case" by Mary Crowley (1993), "Using Students' Portfolios to Assess Mathematical Understanding" by Harold Asturias (1994), and "Portfolio Assessment: Making It Work the First Time" by Therese Kuhs (1994).*

Few high school students are familiar with portfolios as a way to assess mathematics. In **figure 3.17** is a letter written by a teacher to her students to prepare them to use this new and unfamiliar assessment tool.

FIG. 3.17

STUDENT LETTER ABOUT PORTFOLIOS

Term Portfolio

The main purpose of this portfolio is to showcase your best work this term. The most important benefit of this activity is to have you think about what you have learned. I hope that the process of assembling the portfolio will help you gain an honest understanding of what you have learned.

You are to select problems you have done this quarter in whose solutions you have addressed the broad goals of the course. You may select problems from homework, tests, extended take-home problems, or in-class explorations.

For each piece selected, attach a paragraph that accomplishes the following:

1) Explains why you selected the piece

2) Explains how that piece shows you have addressed a specific goal

Before turning in your portfolio, complete the checklist below:

___ Table of contents completed

___ Paragraph for each piece written and attached

___ A piece of work submitted for each broad goal of the course (see below)

___ A piece of work submitted for each specific goal of the course

BROAD GOALS OF COURSE

■ You justify your work so that others understand what you did.

■ You use problem-solving strategies to solve problems unlike the ones done in class.

■ You communicate mathematically.

■ You make connections among different types of mathematics or with different subjects.

CHAPTER 3

Collecting Evidence through Portfolios

Checklists can be developed to help students put their portfolios together. In **figures 3.18** and **3.19** are two examples.

FIG. 3.18

PORTFOLIO GRADE SHEET

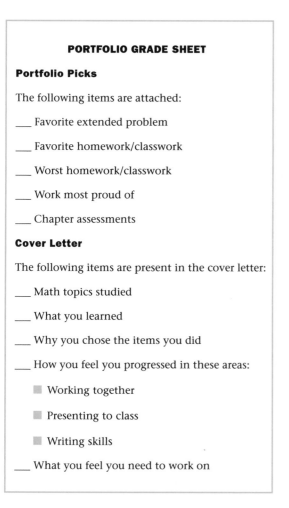

PORTFOLIO GRADE SHEET

Portfolio Picks

The following items are attached:

___ Favorite extended problem

___ Favorite homework/classwork

___ Worst homework/classwork

___ Work most proud of

___ Chapter assessments

Cover Letter

The following items are present in the cover letter:

___ Math topics studied

___ What you learned

___ Why you chose the items you did

___ How you feel you progressed in these areas:

▪ Working together

▪ Presenting to class

▪ Writing skills

___ What you feel you need to work on

FIG. 3.19

PORTFOLIO EVALUATION

PORTFOLIO ASSESSMENT

The primary purpose of this portfolio is to highlight your best performance in mathematics this year. Carefully select the entries for your portfolio so that the criteria in the checklist below are met. Use the checklist to make sure that your portfolio is complete.

Contents

_____ Cover sheet with name, teacher, class, date

_____ Letter to the reviewer

_____ Table of contents

_____ Required number of entries (5–7)

_____ Required reflection pieces

Communication Skills

_____ Entries are organized in a purposeful way.

_____ Entries are legible to readers.

_____ Entries use tables, pictures, charts, and graphs to communicate.

_____ Entries use correct mathematics vocabulary.

Technology Skills

_____ Entries show appropriate use of technology.

_____ Entries show expertise with technology.

Problem-Solving and Reasoning Skills

_____ Entries show problems that were approached logically.

_____ Entries show the use of a variety of problem-solving strategies.

_____ Entries show real-world applications of mathematics.

CHAPTER *3*

Collecting Evidence through Portfolios

On the right are some management tips from teachers who have experience with portfolios. In **figure 3.20** is an exemplary portfolio completed for the Kentucky state assessment system. It includes a letter to the reader and five entries. Note the detail and the use of equations, graphs, and tables in the student's explanations. Also note how technology played an important role in developing the portfolio.

FIG. 3.20

SAMPLE PORTFOLIO

TABLE OF CONTENTS

Letter to the Reviewer

1. Investment Plan
2. Effects of Changing Values
3. Park Clean-Up Problem
4. Minimum Tracking Problem

Dear Reviewer,

This portfolio contains the best examples of my work in mathematics throughout all four of my high school years. These five pieces have been carefully revised and a great quantity of time has been put into their construction. These pieces have expanded my knowledge of math, therefore I have grown as a student.

I feel the best example of my work is Investment Plan, which is a plan I devised for Ms. I. Juana Berich. She wanted to save $20,000.00 in the least amount of time through bank and savings accounts. Investment Plan helped me learn things about banking and interests rates that I had never known. I found out how low, medium, and high risks work and about programs like savings accounts and CD's. I feel I explained and presented these programs well in Investment Plan. I also find this piece the most interesting, because of the complicated issues it addresses.

I feel I learned the most from Effects of Changing Values. This entry stated the effects of a, b, c, and d in the graph of $f(x)=c+a \sin(bx-d)$. The discovery of the effects of these variables have been used throughout the year in my Pre-Calculus class. I have applied the effects into many of my lessons. I now feel secure in the process of the changing effects of a, b, c, and d.

I am pleased with the final draft of my portfolio. I feel I have learned math through my portfolio that I will use throughout my life. Investment Plan and Effects of Changing Values are two of my favorite pieces. I feel secure about the math I have learned from my portfolio and hopefully this shows through my pieces. I hope you enjoy my portfolio and I thank you for your time.

TIPS FROM TEACHERS

■ *Provide students a structure to follow and suggest themes such as "What I Have Learned about the Big Ideas of the Course" or "How I Have Met the Long-Term Goals of Algebra 1."*

■ *Establish with students a table of contents for the portfolio.*

■ *Have students write a "Letter to the Reader" introducing and justifying the contents.*

■ *Score the portfolios and use the result as a grade in the marking period.*

■ *Have a place to store the portfolios in the classroom where students have easy access to them.*

<u>Investment Plan</u>

Dear Ms. I Juana Berich,

I talked to D   P.   who works at The Stock Yards Bank, to help me devise your best plan. To invest your money to get $20,000.00 in the least amount of time I would suggest a mixture of plans. This way you have more money coming in then if you invested into one single program. My suggestion is a combination of savings accounts, CD's, and an equity mutual fund. These programs are a mixture of low and medium risks, because I feel high risks are too risky. I used a calculator to figure out your investments and profits.

Since you are making $300.00 per month, I divided it up to allow you to have money for yourself. I plan that you will spend:

$30.00 per month for gas

$50.00 per month for clothes

$20.00 per month for miscellanous

$50.00 per month for recreation

This allows you to invest $150.00 per month into the bank. You must start with a savings account at a low risk, because you have so little to invest. A savings account yields 2.5% interest per year. A CD yields 4.5% interest per year, but you must invest $500.00 and it cannot be touched for six months. So, first you must earn $600.00 with a savings account to invest $500.00 in a CD. This means that during the six months your CD is locked in, your savings account is also growing because you leave $100.00 in it. Let me show you

what I mean. I used this equation:

$$A=\frac{P(e^{-1})}{e^{i-1}-1}$$

$$600=\frac{150(e^{-1}-1)}{e^{-.025\times2}-1}$$

$$600=\frac{150(e^{-t}-1)}{(.002085505)}\quad .002085505$$

$$\frac{1.2513029}{150}=\frac{150(e^{-t}-1)}{150}$$

$$.008340199=e -1$$
$$\underline{+1\qquad +1}$$
$$1.0083420199=e$$
$$log_e 1.0083420199=.025t$$

$$\frac{\ln 1.0083420199}{.025}=\frac{.025t}{.025}$$
$$t=.3322967061$$

So, it will take you about four months to get $600.00. I plan for you to take $500.00 and invest in a CD for six months. At the same time deep $100.00 in you savings account and invest $150.00 monthly.

To find the amount in the CD I used the equation A=P(e). I used (1/2) because of six months.

$$A=500(e^{.045\times\frac{1}{2}})$$
$$A=$511.38 \text{ per six months}$$

While at the same time your savings account is also bringing in money. I divided 100 by 6 for your monthly investment.

$$\left(\frac{100}{6}+150\right)\left(\frac{e^{.025\times.5}-1}{e^{.025/6}-1}\right)=$1005.19$$

To start your second CD I took $100.00 out of $1005.19 so I could put it back into the savings account. I then added $995.19 to $511.38 (profit from first CD) and invested it in the second CD.

$$A=$1506.37(e^{.045\times.5})=$1540.65$$

I then repeated the process two more times. I have made a chart of the organized information.

	Amount invested in SA (2.5%)	Amount Collected	Amount invested in CD (4.5%)	Amount Collected
First four months	$150.00	$600.00		
First six months	$166.66	$1005.19	$500.00	$511.38
Second six months	$166.66	$1005.19	$1506.57	$1540.85
Third six months	$166.66	$1005.19	$2536.04	$2593.75
Fourth six months	$166.66	$1005.19	$3531.23	$3611.58

This means that at the end of two years and four months you have made $3611.58. Now you have enough to move on to the meduim risk, where I suggest an equity mutual fund with an interest of 9%. To find the amount needed to reach your goal I used the equation $A=\frac{P(e^{t}-1)}{e^{i/12}-1}$. I divided $3611.58 by 12 to find your monthly rate.

$$P=\frac{3611.58}{12}+150=$450.97 \text{ monthly rate}$$

$$20,000=\frac{450.97(e^{.09t}-1)}{e^{.09/12}-1}$$

$$\left(20,000=\frac{450.97(e^{.09t}-1)}{.0075281954}\right).0075281954$$

$$\frac{150.5639089}{450.97}=\frac{450.97(e^{.09t}-1)}{450.97}$$
$$.3338667958=e^{.09t}-1$$

$$.3338667958=e^{.09t}-1$$
$$\underline{+1\qquad +1}$$
$$1.3338667958=e$$

$$\frac{log_e 1.3338667958}{.09}=\frac{.09t}{.09}$$
$$t=3.200912103$$

So, it takes you about three years and three months. If you add this to the other two years and four months, you will take you five years and seven months to reach your goal of $20,000.00.

When you begin to earn more money I would suggest investing the extra into blue chip stock. Right now the rate is 9%-10% but it is constantly changing because it is high risk. You could easily lose or gain money with this program. This program charges commission, so you must realize you are losing money in this aspect.

It is not reasonable for you to retire early with this plan or really any plan. Although you have saved a very large sum of money, you still need an income. This income is needed for basic, everyday life. You must always be prepared for the unexpected.

I hope this plan has helped you with your decision. It can be done but careful organization and patience is required. I wish you the best of luck!

Sincerely,
Mrs. Moneybags

CHAPTER 3

FIG. 3.20 (Continued)

SAMPLE PORTFOLIO

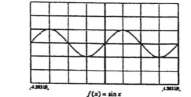

Investigating Shifts and Transformations of Trigonometric Functions

Working with a partner, investigate the effects of changing values of *a*, *b*, *c*, and *d* in the graph of $f(x) = c + a\sin(bx - d)$. You should begin with the basic sine graph and make comparisons. Let $b = 1$ until you have discovered the effects of the others. Be sure to try negative and non-integer values as well as whole number values but use numbers small enough that the standard trig window shows at least one period. Write a coherent summary of your findings. Include sample graphs to illustrate your point. Your work should be clear to *any* junior or senior math student.

$$f(x) = \sin x$$

Effects of Changing Values

To find the effects of changing values of A, B, C, and D in the graph f(x)=c+a sin (bx-d), I began with the basic sine graph. I then took each letter separately and compared their graphs to y=sin x.

To find the effects of C, I used the equations y=2+sin x and y=-2+sin x, compared to y=sin x. The positive value of C shifted y=sin x two points up on the y-axis. The negative value of C shifted y=sin x two points downward on the y-axis.

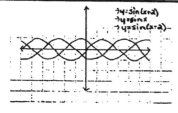

Next I found the effects of D, using the equations y=sin x (x-2) and y=sin (x+2), compared to y=sin x. Y=sin (x-2) shifts y=sin x horizontally two points to the right. Y=sin (x+2) shifts y=sin x horizontally two points to the left.

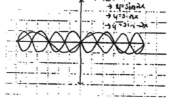

The changing effects of A were a little more complicated. To find these effects, I used y=2sin x and y=-2sin x, when compared to y=sin x. When I graphed y=2sin x, the graph vertically stretched, making the highest point on the y-axis two, therefore the amplitude is two. The graph for y=-2sin x reflects y=2sin x over the x-axis and the amplitude is negative two. All three equations intersect at the same points on the x-axis.

I also put in 1/2 and -1/2 for the amplitude. My results were that the graphs vertically shrink, but the x-intercepts remain the same.

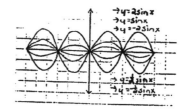

Lastly I found the changing effects of B. To make this discovery I used the equations of y=sin 2x and y=sin (-2x), compared to y=sin x. For both graphs, I found that the period is 1/2 of the period of y=sin x, giving the graphs a shrunken look. Y=sin (-2x) makes a vertical reflection of y=sin 2x over the y-axis, while at the same time the period is reduced by 1/2. All three of these graphs have the same x-intercepts. To stretch the graph of y=sin x, B must be less than one.

In conclusion, by substituting in numbers, I have found the changing effects of A, B, C, and D in the graph of f(x)=c+a sin (bx-d). C makes the graph move up or down, D moves the graph horizontally to the left or right, A vertically stretches or shrinks the graph, and B shrinks or stretches the period. Hence, I can assume that y=3-sin (x+2) moves the graph up three and horizontally shifts it two points to the left. I also know that y=2 sin (5-10x) vertically stretches because of an amplitude of two. It horizontally shrinks the period to five;

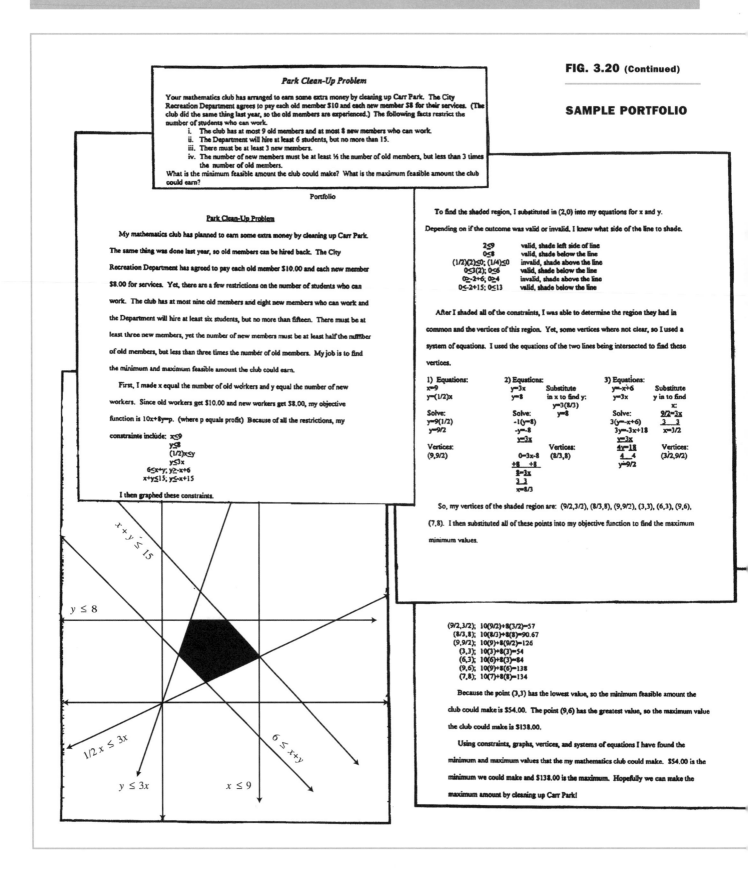

FIG. 3.20 (Continued)

SAMPLE PORTFOLIO

Park Clean-Up Problem

Your mathematics club has arranged to earn some extra money by cleaning up Carr Park. The City Recreation Department agrees to pay each old member $10 and each new member $8 for their services. (The club did the same thing last year, so the old members are experienced.) The following facts restrict the number of students who can work.

  i.   The club has at most 9 old members and at most 8 new members who can work.
  ii. The Department will hire at least 6 students, but no more than 15.
  iii. There must be at least 3 new members.
  iv. The number of new members must be at least ½ the number of old members, but less than 3 times the number of old members.

What is the minimum feasible amount the club could make? What is the maximum feasible amount the club could earn?

Portfolio

Park Clean-Up Problem

My mathematics club has planned to earn some extra money by cleaning up Carr Park. The same thing was done last year, so old members can be hired back. The City Recreation Department has agreed to pay each old member $10.00 and each new member $8.00 for services. Yet, there are a few restrictions on the number of students who can work. The club has at most nine old members and eight new members who can work and the Department will hire at least six students, but no more than fifteen. There must be at least three new members, yet the number of new members must be at least half the number of old members, but less than three times the number of old members. My job is to find the minimum and maximum feasible amount the club could earn.

First, I made x equal the number of old workers and y equal the number of new workers. Since old workers get $10.00 and new workers get $8.00, my objective function is 10x+8y=p. (where p equals profit) Because of all the restrictions, my constraints include: x≤9
y≤8
(1/2)x≤y
y≤3x
6≤x+y; y≥-x+6
x+y≤15; y≤-x+15

I then graphed these constraints.

To find the shaded region, I substituted in (2,0) into my equations for x and y.

Depending on if the outcome was valid or invalid, I knew what side of the line to shade.

2≤9	valid, shade left side of line
0≤8	valid, shade below the line
(1/2)(2)≤0; (1/4)≤0	invalid, shade above the line
0≤3(2); 0≤6	valid, shade below the line
0≥-2+6; 0≥4	invalid, shade above the line
0≤-2+15; 0≤13	valid, shade below the line

After I shaded all of the constraints, I was able to determine the region they had in common and the vertices of this region. Yet, some vertices where not clear, so I used a system of equations. I used the equations of the two lines being intersected to find these vertices.

1) Equations:
x=9
y=(1/2)x

Solve:
y=9(1/2)
y=9/2

Vertices:
(9,9/2)

2) Equations:
y=3x
y=8

Solve:
-1(y=8)
-y=-8
y=3x

0=3x-8
+8   +8
8=3x
3 3
x=8/3

Substitute
in x to find y:
y=3(8/3)
y=8

Vertices:
(8/3,8)

3) Equations:
y=-x+6
y=3x

Solve:
3(y=-x+6)
3y=-3x+18
y=3x
4y=18
4   4
y=9/2

Substitute
y in to find
x:
9/2=3x
3   3
x=3/2

Vertices:
(3/2,9/2)

So, my vertices of the shaded region are: (9/2,3/2), (8/3,8), (9,9/2), (3,3), (6,3), (9,6), (7,8). I then substituted all of these points into my objective function to find the maximum minimum values.

(9/2,3/2); 10(9/2)+8(3/2)=57
(8/3,8); 10(8/3)+8(8)=90.67
(9,9/2); 10(9)+8(9/2)=126
(3,3); 10(3)+8(3)=54
(6,3); 10(6)+8(3)=84
(9,6); 10(9)+8(6)=138
(7,8); 10(7)+8(8)=134

Because the point (3,3) has the lowest value, so the minimum feasible amount the club could make is $54.00. The point (9,6) has the greatest value, so the maximum value the club could make is $138.00.

Using constraints, graphs, vertices, and systems of equations I have found the minimum and maximum values that the my mathematics club could make. $54.00 is the minimum we could make and $138.00 is the maximum. Hopefully we can make the maximum amount by cleaning up Carr Park!

x+y ≤ 15

y ≤ 8

1/2 x ≤ 3x

y ≤ 3x

6 ≤ x+y

x ≤ 9

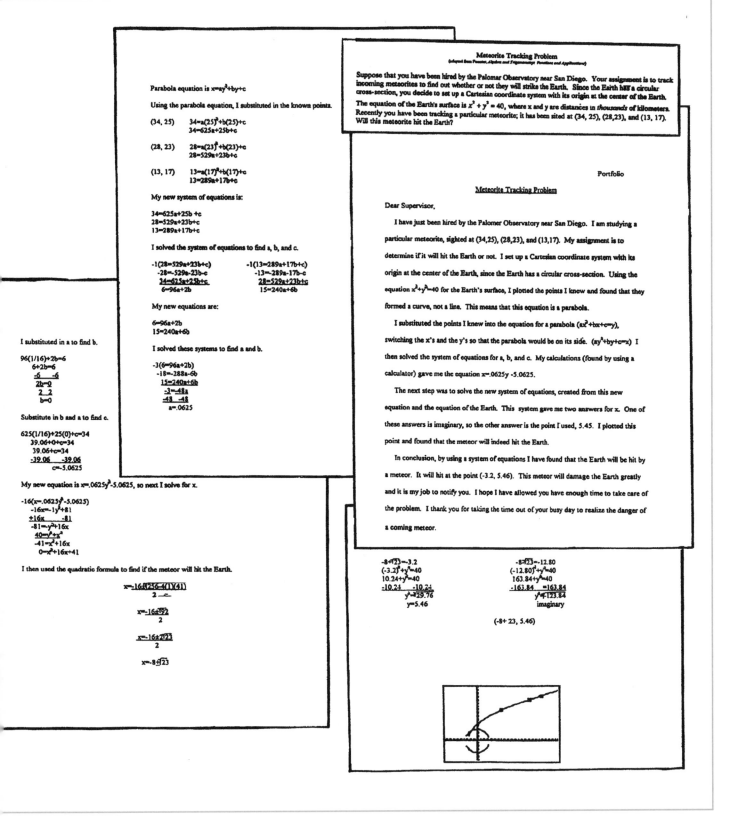

Parabola equation is $x=ay^2+by+c$

Using the parabola equation, I substituted in the known points.

(34, 25) $34=a(25)^2+b(25)+c$
           $34=625a+25b+c$

(28, 23) $28=a(23)^2+b(23)+c$
           $28=529a+23b+c$

(13, 17) $13=a(17)^2+b(17)+c$
           $13=289a+17b+c$

My new system of equations is:

$34=625a+25b+c$
$28=529a+23b+c$
$13=289a+17b+c$

I solved the system of equations to find a, b, and c.

$-1(28=529a+23b+c)$ $-1(13=289a+17b+c)$
$-28=-529a-23b-c$ $-13=-289a-17b-c$
$\underline{34=625a+25b+c}$ $\underline{28=529a+23b+c}$
$6=96a+2b$ $15=240a+6b$

My new equations are:

$6=96a+2b$
$15=240a+6b$

I solved these systems to find a and b.

$-3(6=96a+2b)$
$-18=-288a-6b$
$\underline{15=240a+6b}$
$\underline{-3=-48a}$
$-48\quad-48$
$a=.0625$

I substituted in a to find b.

$96(1/16)+2b=6$
$6+2b=6$
$\underline{-6\quad-6}$
$\underline{2b=0}$
$2\quad2$
$b=0$

Substitute in b and a to find c.

$625(1/16)+25(0)+c=34$
$39.06+0+c=34$
$39.06+c=34$
$\underline{-39.06\quad-39.06}$
$c=-5.0625$

My new equation is $x=.0625y^2-5.0625$, so I solve for x.

$-16(x=.0625y^2-5.0625)$
$-16x=-1y^2+81$
$\underline{+16x\qquad-81}$
$-81=-y^2+16x$
$\underline{40=y^2+x^2}$
$-41=-x^2+16x$
$0=x^2+16x+41$

I then used the quadratic formula to find if the meteor will hit the Earth.

$$x=\frac{-16\pm\sqrt{256-4(1)(41)}}{2}$$

$$x=\frac{-16\pm\sqrt{92}}{2}$$

$$x=\frac{-16\pm2\sqrt{23}}{2}$$

$$x=-8\pm\sqrt{23}$$

Meteorite Tracking Problem
(adapted from Foerster, Algebra and Trigonometry: Functions and Applications)

Suppose that you have been hired by the Palomar Observatory near San Diego. Your assignment is to track incoming meteorites to find out whether or not they will strike the Earth. Since the Earth has a circular cross-section, you decide to set up a Cartesian coordinate system with its origin at the center of the Earth.

The equation of the Earth's surface is $x^2 + y^2 = 40$, where x and y are distances in *thousands* of kilometers. Recently you have been tracking a particular meteorite; it has been sited at (34, 25), (28,23), and (13, 17). Will this meteorite hit the Earth?

Portfolio

Meteorite Tracking Problem

Dear Supervisor,

I have just been hired by the Palomer Observatory near San Diego. I am studying a particular meteorite, sighted at (34,25), (28,23), and (13,17). My assignment is to determine if it will hit the Earth or not. I set up a Cartesian coordinate system with its origin at the center of the Earth, since the Earth has a circular cross-section. Using the equation $x^2+y^2=40$ for the Earth's surface, I plotted the points I knew and found that they formed a curve, not a line. This means that this equation is a parabola.

I substituted the points I knew into the equation for a parabola ($ax^2+bx+c=y$), switching the x's and the y's so that the parabola would be on its side. ($ay^2+by+c=x$) I then solved the system of equations for a, b, and c. My calculations (found by using a calculator) gave me the equation $x=.0625y^2-5.0625$.

The next step was to solve the new system of equations, created from this new equation and the equation of the Earth. This system gave me two answers for x. One of these answers is imaginary, so the other answer is the point I used, 5.45. I plotted this point and found that the meteor will indeed hit the Earth.

In conclusion, by using a system of equations I have found that the Earth will be hit by a meteor. It will hit at the point (-3.2, 5.46). This meteor will damage the Earth greatly and it is my job to notify you. I hope I have allowed you have enough time to take care of the problem. I thank you for taking the time out of your busy day to realize the danger of a coming meteor.

$-8+\sqrt{23}=-3.2$ $-8-\sqrt{23}=-12.80$
$(-3.2)^2+y^2=40$ $(-12.80)^2+y^2=40$
$10.24+y^2=40$ $163.84+y^2=40$
$\underline{-10.24\quad-10.24}$ $\underline{-163.84\quad-163.84}$
$y^2=29.76$ $y^2=-123.84$
$y=5.46$ imaginary

$(-8+23, 5.46)$

Chapter 4

What Do I Do with the Work I Have Collected?

Teacher-to-Teacher

I've become more and more dissatisfied with what I learn about my students from the homework I check and the quizzes and tests I give. Sometimes it seems as if I can predict how they'll do even before I look at their papers. What's the point? And when I get to the end of a grading period, I find it difficult to accept the percents in my grade book as the full story for many of my students. I decided, therefore, to use some new ways to assess my students' understanding. I found a few good open-ended problems that fit my curriculum, and when I collected my students' work on the first one, I was surprised by the number of different approaches they used to solve the problem. I was also surprised by the amount of good mathematics in papers that didn't have a right answer. Because of this, I had a hard time grading the papers. It took me hours to read and make sense of each of the papers and then assign a fair grade. I've gotten better with practice, but it still takes a lot of time, and the students' self-assessments often don't seem very thoughtful or accurate. Recently, I assigned a good problem as a group project. There were fewer papers to grade, but it seemed as if each group complained—for different reasons— about having to share the grade on the paper. Now I'm at the end of another semester. How do I use this new evidence? It looks as if I'm going to have percents again, and now I'm even more uneasy about their meaning.

Scoring Student Work

HOW DO SCORING AND GRADING DIFFER?

Throughout this book, we have used the word *assessment* to mean the process of gathering evidence about what students know and are able to do. We now introduce the term *evaluation* to mean the process of making judgments, or placing value, on the evidence.

The two most common methods of making these judgments are *scoring* and *grading*. On the one hand, scoring is comparing student work to a standard. The standards are designed to communicate our expectations for student work and provide us with a structure for reliably and accurately scoring that work. Scoring student work then becomes an evaluation—placing a value on a piece of evidence. Grading, on the other hand, is what we do with a set of scores to summarize student performance and communicate it to others.

For example, judges score the routine of a gymnast against a set of well-articulated criteria that describe levels of performance. The scores are reliable when they are accurate and consistent measures of the performance according to standards. If a judge takes into account who performed or the circumstances of the performance, the resulting relative score, or grade, is a less accurate measure of the performance itself. The grade, however, might be a more meaningful report of the performance if we view it in the context of reasonable expectations of the performer. For example, a score of 5 on a floor exercise routine could be a D (for an intercollegiate competitor) or an A (for an eight-year-old) (Wiggins 1996).

When we collect students' performances on assessment items, our first task is to score those performances against well-defined sets of criteria that describe levels of performance. Armed with these and other standards-based assessment tools, we can assign grades (and create other reports) using our judgment about students' performance according to our expectations for achievement in context and our expectations for growth over time.

WHAT IS A RUBRIC?

For practical purposes, we will define a *rubric* to mean a hierarchy of standards used to score student work. Rubrics help us keep the focus of our assessment on performance rather than on the performer. We use rubrics to assign scores to student work—most often on a 4-, 5-, or 6-point scale.

Well-designed rubrics allow students to see descriptions of the requirements for their performance. Teachers who have successfully used rubrics report that their students produce higher-quality work when they know the rubric used for scoring.

WHAT TYPES OF RUBRICS ARE AVAILABLE?

Teachers use two types of rubrics in scoring mathematics performance: **holistic** rubrics and **analytic** rubrics. Holistic rubrics capture the overall quality of students' performance on an assessment item. They generally specify several levels of overall performance along with a list of features that characterize each level.

Scoring Student Work

Analytic rubrics are used when performance on a task is viewed from several different perspectives or is broken into several important components. Each of these perspectives or components is then scored separately. The rubrics describe several levels of performance for each of the perspectives or components.

The example in **figure 4.1** shows how holistic and analytic rubrics are used. The "Area Between" task could be given to students in a geometry class.

FIG. 4.1

KIRIS ASSESSMENT TASK GRADE 12
Question 2

Chapter Overview

In this chapter you will read about—

☐ scoring student performance;

☐ summarizing the scores and translating them into grades;

☐ communicating with parents, next year's teachers, colleges, and employers;

☐ making instructional decisions based on evidence of student performance.

GRADES 9-12

READ ABOUT...

■ *Read more about scoring and grading in "Scores and Grades: What Are the Problems? What Are the Alternatives?" by Judith Zawojewski and Richard Lesh (1996).*

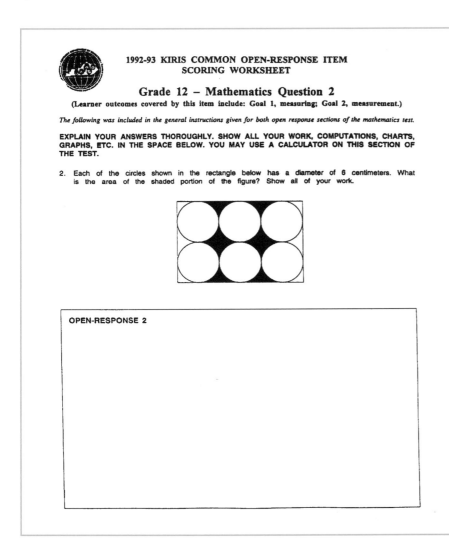

1992-93 KIRIS COMMON OPEN-RESPONSE ITEM
SCORING WORKSHEET

Grade 12 – Mathematics Question 2
(Learner outcomes covered by this item include: Goal 1, measuring; Goal 2, measurement.)

The following was included in the general instructions given for both open response sections of the mathematics test.

EXPLAIN YOUR ANSWERS THOROUGHLY. SHOW ALL YOUR WORK, COMPUTATIONS, CHARTS, GRAPHS, ETC. IN THE SPACE BELOW. YOU MAY USE A CALCULATOR ON THIS SECTION OF THE TEST.

2. Each of the circles shown in the rectangle below has a diameter of 6 centimeters. What is the area of the shaded portion of the figure? Show all of your work.

OPEN-RESPONSE 2

1992-93 KIRIS Common Open–Response Item. Reprinted with permission from the Kentucky Department of Education. Note that KIRIS has been replaced by the Commonwealth Accountability Testing System.

Scoring Student Work

Below is a holistic rubric that might be used to score student work on this task.

HOLISTIC RUBRIC

4   The student answers the question correctly ($144 - 36\pi$ cm^2) or gives an approximation to the answer. The student also describes a correct strategy.

3   The response includes either a correct answer with an incomplete strategy or a complete, correct strategy with an incorrect answer.

2   The strategy displayed is partially correct, showing use of the area of the circle or the area of the rectangle or both.

1   The student's answer is irrelevant, off task, or incorrect. The response may contain some correct computation.

0   Blank.

Below is an analytic rubric that might be used to score student work on the same task.

ANALYTIC RUBRIC

Solution strategy

2   Complete, correct strategy

1   Incomplete strategy, partially correct strategy

0   No strategy offered

Use of circle or rectangle areas

2   Correct use of areas of both circle and rectangle

1   Correct use of area of circle or area of rectangle

0   No evidence of use of areas

Accuracy of computation

2   Correct, accurate computation

1   Only minor computational errors

0   Major computational errors, or computation not attempted

Note how the two rubrics differ in the way points are assigned.

CHAPTER *4*

Scoring Student Work

Figure 4.2 shows a sample of student work.

FIG. 4.2

STUDENT WORK—KIRIS ASSESSMENT TASK

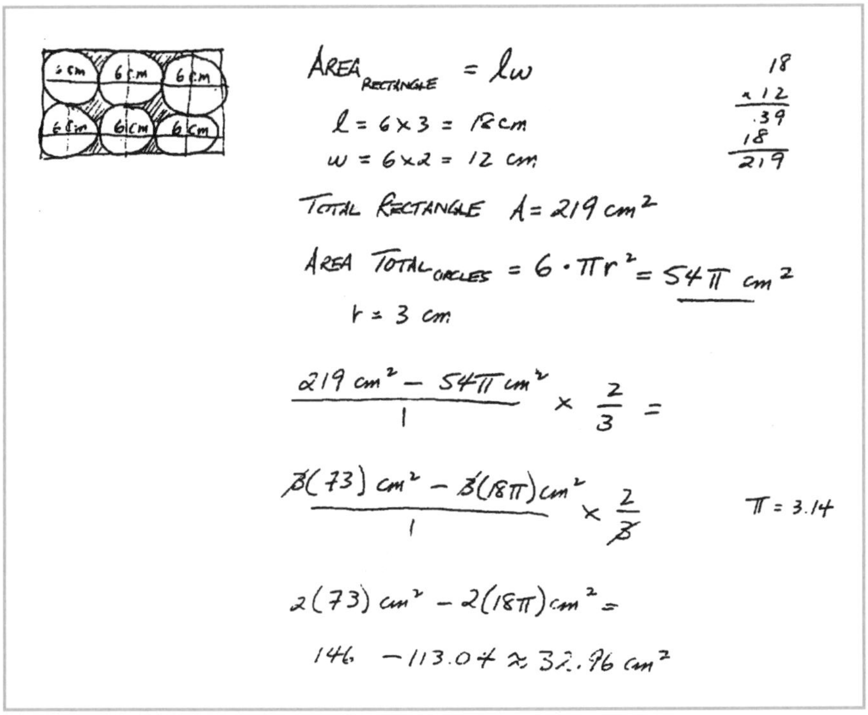

$$\text{AREA}_{\text{RECTANGLE}} = \ell w$$

$$\ell = 6 \times 3 = 18 cm$$
$$w = 6 \times 2 = 12 cm$$

$$\text{TOTAL RECTANGLE} \quad A = 219 cm^2$$

$$\text{AREA TOTAL}_{\text{ORCLES}} = 6 \cdot \pi r^2 = 54\pi \ cm^2$$
$$r = 3 cm$$

$$\frac{219 cm^2 - 54\pi \ cm^2}{1} \times \frac{2}{3} =$$

$$\frac{3(73) cm^2 - 3(18\pi) cm^2}{1} \times \frac{2}{3} \qquad \pi = 3.14$$

$$2(73) cm^2 - 2(18\pi) cm^2 =$$

$$146 - 113.04 \approx 32.96 cm^2$$

$$\begin{array}{r} 18 \\ \times 12 \\ \hline .39 \\ 18 \\ \hline 219 \end{array}$$

1992-93 KIRIS Common Open–Response Item. Reprinted with permission from the Kentucky Department of Education. Note that KIRIS has been replaced by the Commonwealth Accountability Testing System.

Below are scores and rationales derived from the holistic rubric and the analytic rubric.

Holistic Score and Rationale

Overall Score: 3

Rationale: Complete, correct strategy (find overall area, subtract circle areas, take two-thirds of result) with an incorrect answer (minor computational error—18 × 12).

Analytic Score and Rationale

Strategy: 2; Use of areas: 2; Computation: 1

Rationale: Complete, correct strategy (find overall area, subtract circle areas, take two-thirds of result) with an incorrect answer (minor computational error—18 × 12).

Scoring Student Work

Holistic and analytic rubrics can be written as general criteria and can be applied to many different tasks. **Figures 4.3 and 4.4** provide an example of a general holistic rubric and an analytic rubric.

FIG. 4.3

HOLISTIC SCORING RUBRIC

GENERIC ON-DEMAND RUBRIC

"4", "5" Accomplishes the task.

The response accomplishes the prompted purpose. The student's strategy and execution are at a performance level consonant with the relevant standards cluster (skills, conceptual understanding, or problem solving and communication), and qualitative demands of the task. Even for tasks that are very open regarding content, the content chosen by the student must serve the purpose well. Communication is judged by its effectiveness, not by grammatical correctness or length.

Although a "4" need not be perfect, any defects must be minor and very likely to be repaired by the student's own editing, without benefit of a note from a reader.

Distinguished performances are nominated for "Distinguished Performance" recognition, the "5." A distinguished performance is exciting—a gem. It excels and merits nomination for distinction by meeting the standard for a "4" and demonstrating special insights or powerful generalizations or eloquence or other exceptional qualities. A score of "5" is not applicable for every task

"3" Ready for Needed Revision.

Evidence in the response convinces you that the student can revise the work to a "4" with the help of written feedback. The student does not need a dialogue or additional teaching. Any overlooked issues, misleading assumptions, or errors in execution—to be addressed in the revision—do not subvert the scorer's confidence that the student's mathematical power is ample to accomplish the task.

"2" Partial success.

Part of the task is accomplished, but there is a lack of evidence—or evidence of lack—in some areas needed to accomplish the whole task. It is not clear that the student is ready to revise the work without a conversation or more teaching.

"1" Engaged task with little success.

The response may have fragments of appropriate material from the curriculum, and may show effort to accomplish the task, but with little or no success. The task may be misconceived, or the approach may be incoherent, or the response might lack any correct results. Nonetheless, it is evident that the respondent tackled the task and put some mathematical knowledge and tools to work.

0 No response or off task.

When the response is blank, it is scored an "NR" (no response). When there are marks, words or drawings unrelated to the task, it is scored "OT" (off task). In either case, there is no evidence that the task was engaged.

Reprinted with permission from New Standards™. The New Standards™ assessment system includes performance standards with performance descriptions, student work samples and commentaries, on-demand examinations and a portfolio system. For more information contact the National Center on Education and the Economy, 202-783-3668 or www.ncee.org.

Scoring Student Work

FIG. 4.4

ANALYTIC SCORING RUBRIC

MEETS EXPECTATIONS

UNDERSTANDING
- I understand the problem.
- I have spent enough time working on it to come to a conclusion, or I have really good questions.
- If this is an investigation, I have tried several different approaches.

MATHEMATICS
- I understand, **_or am developing an understanding of_**, the mathematics in the assignment.
- Based on my investigation, I have made reasonable conclusions, conjectures and/or _questions_.

COMMUNICATION
- I have told you or showed you how I got my answer.
- If I don't have an answer yet, you can see what I am thinking about. **_This may include questions that I have at this point._**
- I probably used pictures, drawings, diagrams, graphs, numbers, or tables to explain how I did the problem.

EXCEEDS EXPECTATIONS

UNDERSTANDING
- I got it! I understand the problem and I have really investigated it. In doing so, I have probably taken it to a higher level.

MATHEMATICS
- I understand the problem in greater depth or I have extended the problem in some way.
- Based on the investigation, I have made correct conclusions and/or appropriate conjectures.
- I have included evidence of understanding the mathematical concepts and procedures, and I may give evidence of mathematical insight beyond the basic problem.
- I have probably thought about and tried to explain why certain aspects of the problem behave the way they do _in terms of **mathematics**_.

COMMUNICATION
- I very clearly laid out step by step how I solved the problem.
- I proved that my answer is right.
- I may be able to show you another way to arrive at my answer.
- I probably used pictures, drawings, diagrams, graphs, numbers, or tables to show the reader exactly how I thought about the problem.

NO GRADE
- I need to spend some more time working on this problem in order to show an adequate investigation.
- I need to read the feedback questions from the teacher on my work, and do what they say.
- _This assignment must be revised and/or completed, and then re-submitted in order for me to meet or exceed the expectations._

Scorer #1_____

What I really like about this POW is...

Suggestions:

Score (check one):

_____Meets Expectations

_____Exceeds Expectations

_____No Grade

Scorer #2_____

What I really like about this POW is...

Suggestions:

Score (check one):

_____Meets Expectations

_____Exceeds Expectations

_____No Grade

Scoring Student Work

**TIPS FROM TEACHERS IN
DEVELOPING RUBRICS**

■ *Create a two-point rubric—
acceptable and unacceptable. Then
add more categories as you read
through the work.*

■ *Read a few samples of student
work and rank them by performance. Think about what criteria
you used to rank them. Use these
criteria in your rubric.*

■ *Score samples of student work
with a colleague and discuss what
criteria seem important.*

■ *Get students involved in creating
rubrics. Let them read samples of
anonymous work and decide on
important criteria.*

HOW DO I KNOW WHICH TYPE OF RUBRIC TO USE?

Choosing the type of scoring rubric is an important decision. Because holistic rubrics focus on the overall quality of students' work, very different papers can meet the criteria for the same holistic score. Analytic rubrics, however, provide more specific information because each score focuses on a single component of the student's work. The combined score obtained from adding analytical scores does not necessarily measure overall quality. An analytic rubric never addresses how components contribute to a particular level of overall performance.

It is usually best to use holistic rubrics when our primary concern is the over-all quality of the students' work. It is usually best to use analytic rubrics when we wish to collect information on specific components of students' work.

HOW DO I DEVELOP RUBRICS?

When we develop either holistic or analytic rubrics, it is essential that they be aligned with what we consider important. We should state specific criteria to judge a student's performance on a task and weigh the contribution each aspect of that performance makes to the overall quality of the student's work. It is also important not to be so specific that there is no room for novel or unanticipated approaches. For example, if the holistic rubric in **figure 4.3** had specified a particular strategy, the approach taken by this student might not have been scored as correct. Further, because this rubric specifies that a correct solution is required for a score of 4, this student's work would be scored 3.

We must be careful about adding analytic scores to create single, combined scores for the piece of work. For example, on the sample task cited, a student's response could have a combined score of 3 based on three analytic scores of 1, or on analytic scores of 2 (complete strategy), 1 (only rectangle area used correctly), and 0 (major computational errors). The resulting single score loses the detail that is the potential strength of this approach to scoring.

The vignette on the next page describes how a teacher developed a rubric for a task that she found appropriate for her students.

Scoring Student Work

My consumer math class had been studying automobile loans. A car dealer had come to the class to talk about financing a car. Students selected their "perfect" car and had used their knowledge of compound interest to determine loan payments. I wanted to find a task that would allow them to apply what they had learned to a slightly different context. I found the following task from the Kentucky Instructional Results Information System, and it seemed perfect:

The Metro County High School plans to maintain one car for its driver-training program. Each year the school depreciates the value of the car 25% based on its current value. When the value of the driver-training car drops below $3000, the school policy is to buy a new car at the end of that year. The school paid $9200 for the last car that was purchased. It took four years for the value of that car to drop below $3000. At the end of the fourth year, the car was worth $2910.94.

a. The school is considering purchasing a car for $11,800. Using the same depreciation schedule, how many years would it take for the value of the car to drop below $3000? Show your work, including the value of the car at the end of the last year.

b. When the school buys a new car, it turns in the used car to the dealer. The depreciated value of the used car is applied toward the purchase price of the new car. If, over the 15-year period, the school can purchase new cars for the same price, which cars—the ones priced at $11,800 or the ones priced at $9200—would cost the least amount of money? Mathematically justify your answer.

I sat down and worked the problem. I found that the car costing $11,800 would last for five years and that it would cost less to purchase the car costing $9200 for the fifteen-year period.

In creating a rubric, I first thought about what performance was important to me. I wanted students to demonstrate that they understood the problem, to develop a viable strategy for solving the problem, to reach a correct solution based on their findings, to compute correctly (either by paper and pencil or with a calculator), and to communicate their solution clearly. I decided that an analytic rubric would best serve my needs.

For me, the most important criteria were developing a viable strategy and reaching a correct solution—I assigned each of those 3 points. Next, I felt that understanding and communicating the result were important—I assigned them 2 points each. I decided that computing correctly was included in the other criteria, but I chose to assign 1 point if no computational errors were made. I could not bring myself to give a perfect score if the work included even a minor error.

Scoring Student Work

READ ABOUT...

■ *Read about a group of teachers having trouble agreeing on scoring criteria in "A Difference of Opinion" in* Mathematics Assessment: Cases and Discussion Questions for Grades 6–12 *(Bush 1999).*

■ *Read about a teacher who has trouble developing a rubric for scoring student work in "A Scoring Dilemma" in* Mathematics Assessment: Cases and Discussion Questions for Grades 6–12 *(Bush 1999).*

HOW CAN I BE ASSURED THAT I SCORE STUDENT WORK CONSISTENTLY AND RELIABLY?

Scoring samples of student writing and problem-solving performance requires more judgment than scoring tasks that have one right answer. Making sure that our scores reflect judgments that are consistent among students and over time is important if the scores are to be meaningful.

One solution to the problem is to work with other teachers. Scoring student work together will, over time, lead to more consistent and reliable results. Using rubrics that clearly delineate student performance is also helpful.

In the vignette on the opposite page, a teacher uses a "no points" holistic rubric to score student work. This type of rubric treats levels of performance as separate, but not necessarily as equally spaced, categories. The "In Progress" category makes no further distinctions, because it assumes that students will revise their first drafts. The next day's class activity was designed to communicate to students the meaning of the teacher's high standards of performance.

TIPS FROM TEACHERS TO IMPROVE SCORING

■ *Use fewer categories in the rubric. It is easier to be consistent with four categories than it is with ten categories.*

■ *Read several students' responses before developing a rubric. Look for a variety of responses.*

■ *Try not to look at students' names while scoring their work.*

■ *Read quickly through all papers before reading each carefully.*

■ *Have your mathematics department meet regularly to score student work together.*

Scoring Student Work

*Before Ellen assigned the task in **figure 4.1** to her two classes of sophomores, she devised this "no points" rubric (**fig. 4.5**):*

FIG. 4.5

"NO POINTS" HOLISTIC RUBRIC

Holistic Rubric for "Area Between" Task

M (Meets the Standard) - A solution strategy that includes the correct use of circle and rectangle areas to find the area of the shaded region; an answer that is consistent with the strategy and contains no more than minor computational errors.

E (Exceeds the Standard) - Clearly articulated and complete strategy; correct answer with no computational errors.	**I** (In Progress) - Does not meet the criteria for **M** described above. Not scored; feedback provided.

*With this rubric as a guide, she worked her way through the stacks of papers collected from each of her two classes. First, she sorted the papers into two piles. In the left pile went papers that, after a quick reading, seemed at least to meet her standard. In the right pile went papers that would need to be revised in some way. Ellen then went through the left pile to score each of the papers as either **M** or **E**. Finally, she reread the papers in the right pile and provided written feedback in the form of questions.*

*To prepare for her next classes, Ellen selected four papers from each class: one scored **E**, one scored **M**, and two that needed revision for different reasons. She covered up students' names and any scores or feedback, labeled the papers A, B, C, and D, and made eight copies of each paper. Finally, she assembled eight sets of these four sample papers for each class.*

She began her first class the next day by organizing her students into eight groups of three or four students each. She gave each group a set of papers (the set of papers from her other class) and a copy of her rubric and asked the groups to score the sample papers.

When all the groups finished, she and her students had a lengthy discussion of the papers and the scores students gave them. Then she returned their own papers to the students, saying that those who needed to revise their first drafts should have them at the start of class tomorrow.

*Ellen knew that many students were surprised by the quality of the **M** and **E** papers. She hoped this activity communicated the meaning of good work more effectively than describing it herself. Her hope was that the overall quality of work on the next open-ended problem would be higher. She would not repeat this group-scoring activity and suspected that students would remember it when revising work armed only with her feedback questions.*

READ ABOUT...

■ *Read more about using and developing rubrics in "A Room with More than One View" by Jean Stenmark, Pam Beck, and Harold Asturias (1994), in "Assessing Students' Performance on an Extended Problem-Solving Task: A Story from a Japanese Classroom" by Yoshinori Shimizu and Diana Lambdin (1997), and in "Assessing Mathematical Processes: The English Experience" by Malcolm Swan (1996).*

The scores we assign document levels of performance against absolute standards. As in the vignette, these scores provide information for both teachers and their students. The next section of this chapter focuses on ways to summarize and communicate the data we compile about the performance of students in our classes.

Summarizing the Evidence

HOW CAN I BEST SUMMARIZE THE EVIDENCE THAT I HAVE GATHERED?

Many different people need to know the results of our assessments. Students are first on a list that includes their parents or guardians, counselors and other administrators, other teachers (those who teach the students now and those who will in the future), college admissions officers, employment personnel officers, and most important, ourselves. These people require that we make valid, consistent, and unbiased inferences about our students' mathematical knowledge. They also deserve clear, unambiguous reports of these inferences.

One way, and perhaps the most popular way in the past, is to use grades to summarize student performance. We may assign a grade as a letter (A, B, C, ...), a percentage, or a label like "Excellent," "Satisfactory," or "Needs Improvement." The nature of the grade is usually determined by school or district policy. **Figure 4.6** shows a grading scheme developed by a high school teacher.

CHAPTER *4*

Summarizing the Evidence

FIG. 4.6

LETTER GRADE CHARACTERISTICS

A

- Student's participation in class is in accordance with school policy, consistent, and appropriate to the goals of the class.

- Student is self-directed, that is, willing to attempt work independent of teacher support and direction.

- **Student convincingly demonstrates procedural and conceptual knowledge of the mathematics addressed in the course by showing evidence of expected levels of knowledge of all big ideas in all three categories: Formative, Summative, and Observation or by showing evidence of exceeding expected levels in two of the three categories.**

- **Student attempts all ten Problems of the Week and meets expectation on all or if only five are completed, exceeds expectation on at least one and meets expectation on the others.**

- **A portfolio that reflects the characteristics above and shows satisfactory progress toward meeting the crucial outcomes is completed at the end of each unit.**

B

- Student's participation in class is consistent and appropriate to the goals of the class.

- Student is progressing toward becoming an independent learner.

- **Student convincingly demonstrates procedural and conceptual knowledge of the mathematics addressed in the course by showing evidence of expected levels of knowledge of all big ideas in two of the three categories: Formative, Summative, and Observation or by showing evidence of exceeding expected levels in one of the three categories.**

- **Student attempts all ten Problems of the Week and meets expectation on five or exceeds expectation on at least one.**

- **A portfolio that reflects the characteristics above and shows satisfactory progress toward meeting the crucial outcomes is completed at the end of each unit.**

C

- Student's participation is appropriate to the goals of the class.

- Student tends to rely on the teacher to remind him or her of expectations.

- **Student convincingly demonstrates procedural and conceptual knowledge of the mathematics addressed in the course by showing evidence of expected levels of knowledge in all big ideas in one of the three categories: Formative, Summative, and Observation.**

- **Student attempts all Problems of the Week and meets expectation on at least one.**

- **A portfolio that reflects the characteristics above and shows satisfactory progress toward meeting the crucial outcomes is completed at the end of each unit.**

Summarizing the Evidence

Whatever the specific policy, at the end of each grading period in the school calendar, most of us are faced with the task of aggregating the data in our records into a single grade for each student. (Many school systems also allow comments by the teacher to be reported, but because of a lack of space these comments seldom communicate much specific, meaningful information.)

Condensing the complexity of students' performance in a class over at least several months into a single grade has always been a daunting task. It becomes even more daunting, as described in the "Teacher-to-Teacher" note that began this chapter, when we use the assessment tools discussed in chapter 2. The more we broaden our assessment evidence, the less adequate is a single letter grade as a summary of the evidence. Yet most of us still must use letter grades as our primary reporting mechanism. What do we do?

HOW CAN I TRANSFORM THE EVIDENCE I GATHER ABOUT STUDENTS INTO GRADES?

Teachers have developed many strategies for transforming the evidence gathered about students from different forms of assessment into grades. These strategies range from rather simple translations to more complicated systems. We offer two vignettes of teachers who have developed strategies for transforming evidence into grades. One of them also shows how one teacher changed his grading practices over a period of years.

I began changing my assessment practices two years ago. In addition to homework (which I had always done), I began using weekly open-ended response problems and projects instead of tests and quizzes.

When I used homework, quizzes, and tests, I set up a system where all homework grades together added to one test score. I computed the homework grade by dividing the number of homework assignments completed by the number of homework assignments made. I also gave weekly quizzes and combined the scores into one test score. If I had given four tests during a grading period, I transformed homework to another test score, quizzes to another test score, and found the average of the six scores to determine a grade. My grade book included checks for homework and scores for tests and quizzes.

On the surface, my grade book now does not look very different. (See fig. 4.7.) The way that the checks and numbers are used, however, is quite different. Checks still represent completed homework, and I now keep track of how many problems were completed. I do not include homework in the student's grade at all. I view it as a time for practice, but I keep a record so that I can talk to parents about their child's homework record. My grade book still includes scores for open response items and projects, but I have realized that not all activities hold equal weight. For example, a weeklong project may be worth 110 points, whereas a one-hour open response question might be worth 22 points. I allow revisions on work, and students can improve their score on a piece if the revision is better. I have decided that A work in my class exceeds the standards I have set on tasks; B work meets the standards I have set on tasks; C work represents performance below standards on some assignments; D work represents performance below standards on most assignments; and F work represents consistently poor performance on assignments or failure to complete a sufficient number of assignments. I determined beforehand what score represents exceeding, meeting, or falling short of standards for that task. I look at each student's performance on each task and determine his or her grade.

Summarizing the Evidence

FIG. 4.7

SAMPLE GRADE SHEET

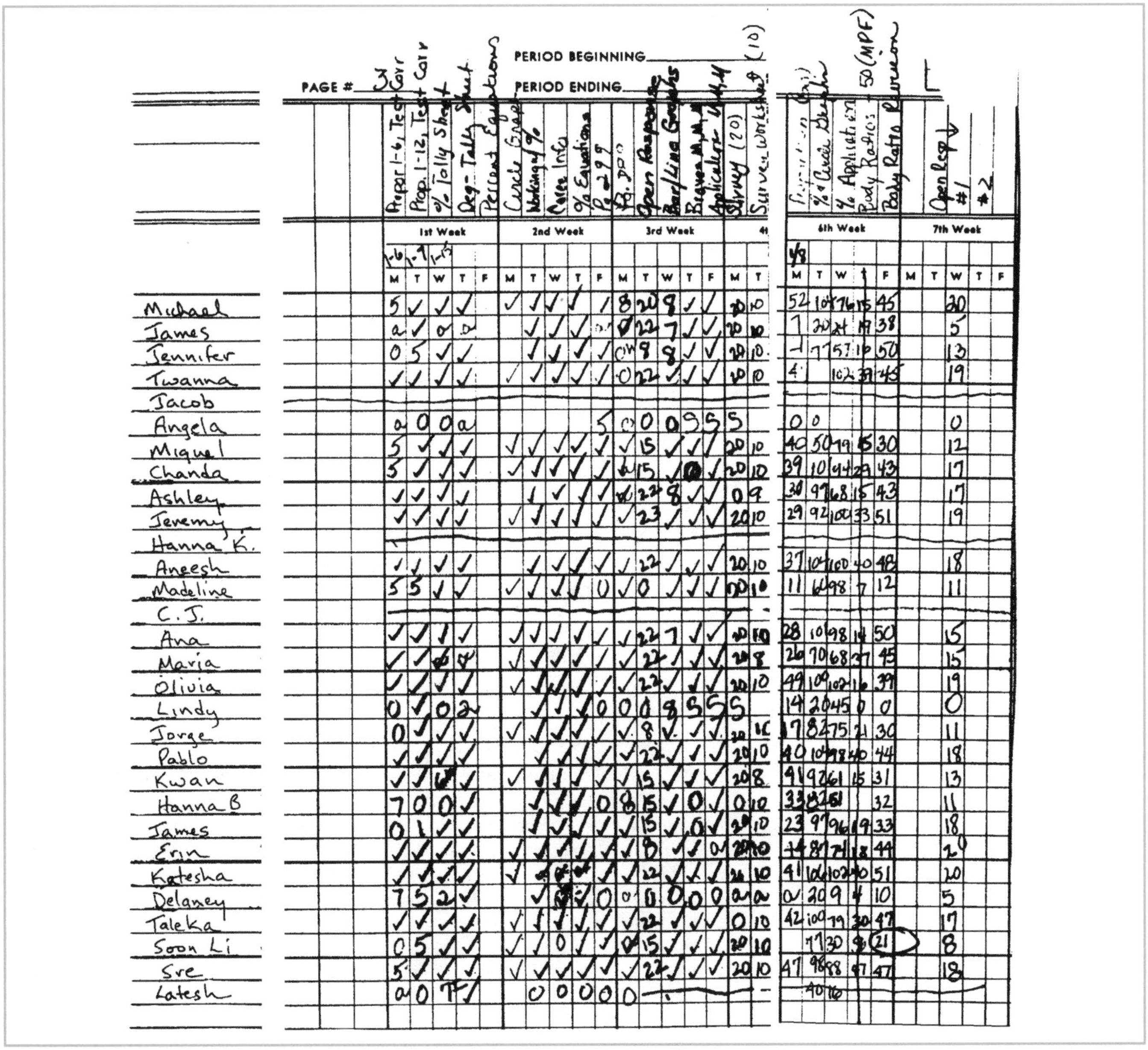

The vignette on the next page shows how a teacher used a matrix of important mathematical ideas in her grading. The development of a meaningful grading scheme is one step in the overall process of planning for assessment. Once we have identified the big mathematical ideas of a class whose work we want to assess, chosen the sources of evidence we will use to assess it, and described the characteristics of work in each grade category, we can use a matrix as a framework for organizing the wealth of assessment data we collect.

Summarizing the Evidence

Chris sat down prior to the start of the new school year and, after some thought and discussion with colleagues, determined that her ninth-grade course centered on five big mathematical ideas. For example, her "Big Idea #1" was "Understand and use linear functions, represented as graphs, tables, and equations." She decided to collect evidence of her students' understanding of her set of big ideas using these five sources:

- *Homework collected periodically*
- *Extended problems—more open tasks assigned once every two weeks (revisions allowed)*
- *In-class work—the quality of participation in groups and in whole-class discussions*
- *Optional projects, with topics determined by students*
- *A comprehensive final exam*

Chris then outlined the following grade criteria. She shared these criteria with her students on the first day of class.

To earn a C, meet the minimum criteria for passing the course. These criteria are—

- *submit all written work;*
- *take the final exam;*
- *meet the standard on at least three of the five big ideas;*
- *miss no more than four classes during the semester.*

To earn a B, meet the criteria for earning a C and provide evidence that you have met the standard on each of the big ideas of the course by meeting the standard on at least one source.

To earn an A, meet the criteria for a B stated above and exceed these standards in at least three of the big ideas. You can exceed the standard in a big idea if you—

- *exceed the standard on at least one source;*
- *meet the standard on more than two sources.*

A student who does not meet the minimum criteria outlined above will receive an F for the course.

---

*Finally, Chris outlined a set of general criteria, or a generic rubric, like the one in **figure 4.4**, to guide the scoring of student work collected from each of these sources. She completed this step before school started, so she could also share the criteria with her students and their parents on the first day of class. In her new grade book, she set up the left page as she always had, with student names down the left-hand column, and columns to record data sequentially. She set up the facing page of her grade book for this course as shown in **figure 4.8**. Using this format, she recorded evidence from each of the five sources (Homework, Extended problems, In-class, Projects, and the Final exam) for each of the big ideas she identified at the start of this process. For example, a student who provided evidence of understanding Big Idea #1—perhaps from responses to homework questions or from some in-class discussion documented by the teacher—had entries in the H and I cells of the Big Idea #1 column.*

As the school year progressed, the various cells of this table began to fill with the accumulated evidence gathered from that student. The entries in the columns on the right side of this teacher's grade book, taken together, provide a five-dimensional picture of the student's demonstrated understanding of each of the big ideas of this course. Finally, the grading criteria she shared with students at the start of the year allowed her to determine grades for each student without using a calculator.

CHAPTER *4*

Summarizing the Evidence

FIG. 4.8

CHRIS'S GRADE BOOK

Big Idea #1					Big Idea #2					Big Idea #3					Big Idea #4					Big Idea #5					Grade
H	E	I	P	F	H	E	I	P	F	H	E	I	P	F	H	E	I	P	F	H	E	I	P	F	

In each of these grading schemes, note how the teachers set important standards—the first teacher for each task and the second teacher for the course as a whole. Assigning grades was slightly different for each teacher, but each had a wealth of evidence about students to share with others.

WHAT PROBLEMS ARISE WHEN WE COMBINE SCORES TO ARRIVE AT GRADES?

Two issues arise when we combine scores into grades. First, when we award partial credit on a quiz or test question, do we consider whether the student who scored 3 points out of 5 actually showed three-fifths of the understanding of the student who scored 5? Did every one of the students who scored 3 show just that much understanding? Did each of the students who scored 4 points out of 5 show twice as much understanding as each of the students who scored 2? On our new 4-point holistic rubric for grading open tasks, does a score of 2 really represent exactly half as much overall quality as a score of 4? Is a score of 3 assigned only to work that falls exactly halfway between those?

The arithmetic we perform on the numerical scores we give—adding, calculating percents, averaging—is valid only if the answer to each of these questions is yes.

The second problem is the independence of different types of assessment information. What does a grade of B mean in our class? Does it mean that the student showed adequate understanding of all the big ideas of the course? Does it mean that the student still has some gaps in understanding but has worked very hard and improved a lot since last semester? Does it mean that the student aced all the tests but did not turn in some of the homework? We might answer yes to all of these. However, if the range of possible meanings for a grade is so great, that grade communicates very little information about any of those aspects of a student's performance. At some point in the process of summarizing assessment data, we are faced with the task of combining types of data that are essentially independent. Some students do almost no homework yet seem to have a solid grasp of the material, whereas other students do their work diligently and continue to struggle with the content. A solid homework record and understanding of the mathematics are, for some students, independent characteristics of their performance in mathematics class in the same way that scoring average and rebounds per game are, for some players, independent characteristics of their basketball performance.

Summarizing the Evidence

READ ABOUT...

Read about a middle school teacher's struggle with grading in "Does This Count for Our Grade?" in Mathematics Assessment: Cases and Discussion Questions for Grades 6–12 *(Bush 1999).*

An assessment scheme such as this one uses a grade book as a database rather than as a spreadsheet. It seems, on the surface, to be more subjective than the more familiar approach that uses the objective results of adding and averaging scores to determine grades based on criteria such as "93%–100% = A." As discussed earlier, these numerical approaches carry little meaning, but a student who earns a B in a class using the approach illustrated in the vignette has met a particular standard of performance on each of the big ideas of the course.

The assessment scheme in the vignette is a big leap from those used in most mathematics classrooms. It might take a series of incremental changes, over several school years, to move from one to the other. "The Evolution of a Grading Scheme" in **figure 4.9** documents one teacher's journey from a familiar approach to assessment to one similar to the one described in the vignette.

FIG. 4.9

EVOLUTION OF A GRADING SCHEME

1991...

Sources of Evidence:

- Homework
- Quizzes
- Final Exam
- Portfolio (A first attempt)

Criteria:

Not specified for students, but points, percentages, and letter grades assigned in the usual manner

---

Grades

- *Homework, quizzes.* Homework will be assigned regularly. I will check frequently to see that it has been done. Both group and individual quizzes, worth varying amounts, will be given periodically. This aspect of your work will constitute 40 percent of your grade.

- *Portfolio.* Each of you will compile a portfolio of your best work. This portfolio should include any material that you think you want me to see, along with written explanations detailing why. This is your chance to ensure that I have all of the information I need to accurately assess your work in this class.

I am particularly interested in the mathematical concepts you develop over the course of the semester, and the processes by which you develop them. Therefore, I am most interested in seeing evidence of this in your portfolios.

...

I will not list all the types of items you might include in your portfolio. I will set only two specific requirements: first, your portfolio must include at least 10 items (less than one per week); second, each item must include a written explanation of what, specifically, I should attend to. Your portfolio will constitute 40 percent of your grade.

- *Cumulative final exam.* Given during the scheduled exam period, this exam will constitute about 20 percent of your grade. It will contribute more if it significantly helps your grade.

Summarizing the Evidence

FIG. 4.9 (Continued)

EVOLUTION OF A GRADING SCHEME

1992...

Grades

- *Homework, quizzes.* Homework will be assigned regularly.... Quizzes, worth varying amounts, will be given periodically. At least four quizzes will be given during the semester. This aspect of your work will constitute 50 percent of your grade.

- *Quiz Revisions.* Each of you will revise each of the quiz questions for which you did not receive full credit.... Your revisions must include some written comments about the mistakes you made, how you corrected them, and what you learned. This will constitute 10 percent of your grade.

- *Exhibits.* Each of you will submit three exhibits, chosen from the work you did in class, or the work you did on out-of-class assignments, that you consider your best work in this course.

...

I will not list all the types of items you might include as exhibits. I will set only three specific requirements: first, you must submit three exhibits; second, each exhibit must include a written explanation of why your submitted it; third, your exhibits are due on, or any time before, the last class meeting. Your exhibits will constitute 20 percent of your grade.

- *Cumulative final exam....* will constitute about 20 percent of your grade. It will contribute more if it significantly helps your grade.

Changes:

- Quizzes and revisions combined into a single source

- CAPs—extended written problems—added as a source of evidence, along with first use of a published set of grading criteria (a three-level rubric)

- Revised weights assigned to sources

Summarizing the Evidence

FIG. 4.9 (Continued)

EVOLUTION OF A GRADING SCHEME

1993...

Changes:

- Quizzes and revisions combined into a single source

- CAPs—extended written problems—added as a source of evidence, along with first use of a published set of grading criteria (a three-level rubric)

- Revised weights assigned to sources

Assessment:

- *Quizzes.* Four quizzes will be given during the semester. Each of you will revise each of the quiz questions for which you did not receive full credit.... Revised quiz grades will constitute about 40 percent of your grade.

- *Collected and Assessed Problems (CAPs).* These problems will be assigned regularly, but no more frequently than once each week. ...

The CAPs will be graded according to the following criteria:

A   Clear and detailed problem statement, process description, and solution, along with either a correct generalization of the solution or extensions to the problem.

B   Satisfactory problem statement, process description, and solution, but no generalizations or extensions. A partial solution to the problem may earn a "B" if the problem statement and process descriptions are clear and detailed and if some extensions to the problem are offered. A CAP write-up that receives a "B" may be revised and resubmitted. (Only the higher grade will count.)

Not Yet   If the minimum criteria for a "B" have not been met, your work will be returned to you with comments and you will be asked to revise and resubmit your work. (Only the higher grade will count.)

CAPs will constitute about 15 percent of your grade.

- *Exhibits....* Your exhibits will constitute about 25 percent of your grade.

- *Cumulative final exam....* will constitute about 20 percent of your grade. It will contribute more if it significantly helps your grade.

1994...

Changes:

- CAPs dropped as a source

- Group write-ups—assessed with three-level rubric used previously for CAPs—added as a source

- Revised weights assigned to sources

Assessment and Grading:

Your semester grade will be determined by assessing your work in both individual and group contexts.

1. *Group work:* Periodically the group in which you are working will be asked to submit a write-up of its work on a problem. Each member of the group will share the grade earned by this write-up. The criteria that will be applied to group work are outlined on the attached sheet. (The first group assignment will be critiqued by me, but no grade will be recorded.) Group write-up grades will constitute 30 percent of your semester grade.

2. *Individual work:*

- *Quizzes and tests....* Quizzes will constitute 35 percent of your semester grade.

- A comprehensive final exam ... will constitute about 20 percent of your semester grade.

- Exhibits. The second type of individual work is a set of two exhibits of your own choosing.... Your exhibits will constitute about 15 percent of your grade.

CHAPTER *4*

Summarizing the Evidence

FIG. 4.9 (Continued)

EVOLUTION OF A GRADING SCHEME

1995...

Assessment and Grading:

- Collected and Assessed Problems (CAPs): ...

- In-Class Work: Preparation for class (including homework), quality of participation in groups and in whole-class discussions, attendance. See description below.

- Final Exam: ...

- Exhibits: ...

The components listed above will be combined, using the following scheme, to determine your final grade.

Changes:

- Group write-ups out and CAPs back as a source, with a revised E-M-IP rubric

- In-class work assesed for the first time (whole-class participation coded by teacher; group work assessed by students)

Components	A	B	C	F
CAP Assessments	All CAPs at least M; more than half at E	All CAPs at least M	No more than 1/3 of CAPs below M	More than 1/3 of CAPs below M
In-Class Work	Whole-Class at E and Group at M for each time period	Whole-Class at M and group at M for at most one time period, —or— Whole-Class at E and Group below M for two time periods	Not at B level, but level of F	Whole-Class below M and Group below M over half the time
Exhibits	Two exhibits at E, or one at E and one at M	Both exhibits at M	Both submitted, but one or more not at M	One or more not submitted
Final Exam (Each problem graded using CAP rubric)	All problems at least M; more than half at E	All problems at least M	No more than 1/3 of problems below M	More than 1/3 of problems below M

- See separate rubrics for the criteria for meeting (M) or exceeding (E) the standards for each component.

- Students must have at least a B in CAP Assessments, and no components at F, in order to get a B in the course.

- Students can earn an A in the course with at least a B in CAP Assessments and an A in at least two other components.

- The four components are listed roughly in the order of their importance in determining final grades, with CAPs most important, in-class work next, followed by exhibits and final exam (weighted equally).

- Percentage weights dropped, in favor of this list of characteristics

Summarizing the Evidence

FIG. 4.9 (Continued)

EVOLUTION OF A GRADING SCHEME

1996...

Changes:

- In-class work (whole-class discussions only) coded by teacher using scheme on p. 109

- No attempt to assign a grade to each source of evidence

- More specific characteristics for aggregating sources of evidence

---

Assessment and Grading:

I will assess your understanding of the big ideas of the course using these sources of evidence:

- Collected and Assessed Problems (CAPs): ...

- In-Class Work: ...

- Exhibits: ...

- Final Exam: ...

I will use the following scheme to determine final grades for the course:

1) A student must meet the standard on each of the big ideas of the course in order to earn a grade of "B":

- The most straightforward way to demonstrate this is for all CAPs to be at M or better, and to earn at least a "C" on the comprehensive final exam. The CAPs I assign will be chosen so that, taken together, they span the big ideas of the course.

- In-class participation, exhibits, and final exam answers may be used to provide evidence not present in CAP write-ups.

2) A student who meets the criteria for a "B" stated above may earn an "A" by exceeding these standards in at least two of the four sources of evidence. Here are some examples:

- At least half of all CAPs at the level of "E," and at least a "B" on the comprehensive final exam

- Some CAPs at the level of "E" and a consistently-high level of class participation

- Some CAPs at "E" and an "A" on the comprehensive final exam

- A consistently high level of class participation and an "A" on the comprehensive final exam

- An exhibit that shows knowledge of one or more of the big ideas beyond the standard, and "A" characteristics in one other area

3) A student who does not meet the criteria for a "B" stated above, but who meets the following minimum criteria for passing this course, will receive a "C" for the semester:

- Miss no more than four classes during the semester

- Submit all written work

- Take the final exam

- Meet the standard on at least two-thirds of all written work (CAPs, final exam questions)

4) A student who does not meet the minimum criteria outlined in (3) will receive an "F" for the course.

Making Instructional Decisions

HOW CAN I USE ASSESSMENT RESULTS TO MAKE INSTRUCTIONAL DECISIONS?

We make instructional decisions many times during each of our classes and as we prepare for a class, a unit, a semester, or a year. Assessment results contribute to these important instructional decisions. Below are a series of questions that we can ask ourselves to guide our decisions. The questions are organized in two groups. The first group helps us decide what activities, questions, or tasks would be appropriate given the present state of our students' knowledge. These decisions affect the *direction* of instruction.

Have I gathered enough information to make instructional decisions at this time?

▪ If not, what can I do to gather more evidence?

▪ If so—

- how many students have already met my standard for understanding at this time? What mathematics do they understand?

- of the students who have not yet met my standards, how many are ready to benefit from the mathematics that comes next?

- do enough students understand enough mathematics to make new activities worthwhile?

- what mathematical activities would be the most beneficial at this time?

▪ Do I have any evidence of what students already know about the activity that comes next?

These questions help us focus our attention on the development of student understanding over time. They assume that understanding is complex and develops differently and at different rates for each student in our classes. They also assume that a student is never "done" with a mathematical concept but that there is a point at which new activities would be beneficial. Those new activities could be—

▪ individual reflection on work done so far;

▪ small- or large-group discussions about solutions and strategies;

▪ different, but related, mathematical tasks.

Making Instructional Decisions

READ ABOUT...

■ *Read about how a teacher uses assessment results to guide his teaching in "The Next Instructional Move" in* Mathematics Assessment: Cases and Discussion Questions for Grades 6–12 *(Bush 1999).*

■ *Read more about using assessment results to make decisions in "Using the Assessment of Students' Learning to Reshape Teaching" by Sandra Wilcox and Ronald Zielinski (1997) and "Seamless Assessment/Instruction = Good Teaching" by Diana Lambdin and Clare Forseth (1996).*

The second group of questions helps us to evaluate how well our lessons achieved our goals. These are decisions about the *effectiveness* of instruction.

Have I gathered enough information to make instructional decisions at this time?

■ If not, what can I do to gather more evidence?

■ If so—

■ how many students were engaged in the tasks I set?

■ for how many students were the tasks mathematically engaging?

■ how many students offered ideas, responded to the ideas of others, or raised questions?

■ with how many students did I interact?

■ for how many students did my instruction not accomplish the goals I set?

■ according to the data I have, were my goals reasonable?

These questions focus on the reasonableness of our instructional plan and on how well we have carried out that plan. They assume that students engaged in authentic problem-solving activities will have many questions. We can expect students not to know what to do; this is not necessarily an indication that something has gone wrong with the lesson. However, the kinds of questions students ask can tell us much about their mathematical understanding.

Communicating to Parents

HOW CAN I BEST COMMUNICATE ASSESSMENT RESULTS TO PARENTS?

Although grading is the most common way to communicate student achievement and progress, it is not the only way. We can also communicate to parents and others through conferences. These conferences allow us to avoid the loss of information inherent in single, summative grades as well as give us opportunities to share with others the independent components of our students' performance. The student's work, set against a backdrop of the course's big ideas and well-articulated standards of performance, makes the information much more meaningful. Unfortunately, most parents are unfamiliar with the types of assessment discussed in this book. It is important that we give them the opportunity to understand the changes occurring at the classroom, state or provincial, and national levels. Here are some suggestions offered by teachers who have been successful in communicating with parents.

Figure 4.10 shows an example of a parent letter written to communicate a teacher's expectations for her students, as well as expectations for the parents.

CHAPTER 4

Communicating to Parents

FIG. 4.10

PARENT LETTER

Dear Parents/Guardians:

As we begin this school year, I want to share with you some insights into what is happening in our math classroom. Communication between home and school is very important for you and especially your son or daughter.

Since it seems things are a bit different since you and I were in school, I would like to share some of the goals for the class and expectations that I have of your son or daughter.

Here are the goals:

1. To communicate mathematically through

- representation (graphs, diagrams, charts, tables, etc.)
- math language
- clear presentation of work

2. To demonstrate problem solving by

- showing an understanding of the tasks
- using approaches, sometimes more than one, that show good, sound mathematical thinking
- explaining decisions along the way
- connecting, extending, applying, and generalizing answers

3. To develop number sense by

- assessing when an answer is reasonable
- using mental strategies to do computation and estimation

4. To understand and apply math skills and concepts

5. To solve problems cooperatively

6. To apply math outside the classroom

7. To use technology to facilitate problem solving

8. To grow in self-esteem and self-confidence as a person and as a mathematician

Continued on next page

TIPS FROM TEACHERS

■ *Let parents know specific goals for assessment. At the beginning of the year send home a letter that communicates your expectations.*

■ *Explain the type of homework you will be giving and show parents examples of open-ended questions or projects their children might bring home.*

■ *Describe your grading system to the parents, since it will probably be quite different from the ones they had in school.*

■ *Provide a specific list of suggestions explaining how parents can help their children with assignments.*

■ *Have students make presentations to their parents about what they know and can do.*

Communicating to Parents

FIG. 4.10 (Continued)

PARENT LETTER

Here are the expectations:

1. Daily homework should take between 20 and 40 minutes (some shorter, some longer). You should be able to say, "That's enough" and write a brief note saying that you believed your son or daughter had spent adequate time.

2. The homework is not traditional textbook homework but questions that require a lot of thought and explanation on the part of the student.

3. I expect that sometimes your son or daughter will get frustrated. I am trying to teach him or her that math is not always an "answer" but a thought process and that sometimes the work turned in might be methods tried that didn't necessarily work or questions that he or she might have in order to get further in the problem.

4. Tests and quizzes are given about once every two weeks.

5. Journal entries will be due on the off-test weeks.

6. Your child (a) will learn to score his or her own work and assess himself or herself and (b) will then discuss a grade for each marking period with me.

Here are some suggestions that will enable you to share in your child's experiences in learning mathematics and help you to create an environment in your home that provides encouragement for your child.

1. Show interest in your child's experience in math class. Ask him or her to tell you about class activities.

2. Ask your child to explain the concepts and relationships he or she is studying. Be concerned with the process as well as the answer. Let your child explain her or his thoughts to you often.

3. When your child has a question, try not to tell how to solve the problem. Ask questions that will help your child to think about the problem in a different way.

4. Encourage your child to draw diagrams, models, or sketches to help explain or understand a concept or problem.

5. Provide a special time or place for study that will not be disrupted by other household activities.

6. Encourage your child to form study groups with classmates. From discussing with others, rich insights will emerge.

7. Engage your child in home activities that draw on a variety of mathematical skills. Games and puzzles, estimations, and math talk at mealtime are good ways to do this.

8. Come and visit your child's math class.

The goals and expectations are strongly related to the National Council of Teachers of Mathematics Curriculum Standards. Teaching math where kids are involved in the process makes math more meaningful and useful. Students will see that it isn't "magic," but they will know why and how things work.

I'm looking forward to seeing you at Open House. Let me know if you have any questions or concerns. I'm excited about the school year ahead and look forward to working with your child.

Sincerely,

Communicating to Parents

Some teachers have had success in having students communicate assessment results to their parents. These student-led conferences are especially beneficial when students are involved in self-assessment in their mathematics classes. They require students to select work to show their parents. The conferences also encourage them to think about the quality of their work and what standards they have met. They provide parents opportunities to see their child's work through the eyes of the child. In **figure 4.11** is a guide that one teacher used to help her students prepare for a parent conference.

READ ABOUT...

■ *Read about parents' reactions to their child's presentation of his mathematics portfolio in "Math Portfolio Night" in* Mathematics Assessment: Cases and Discussion Questions for Grades 6–12 *(Bush 1999).*

FIG. 4.11

GUIDELINES FOR PRESENTING WORK TO PARENTS

Over the next few weeks, each of you will present selected pieces of your mathematics work to your parents or family. The suggestions below are intended to help make your presentation a positive experience. You are to have your presentation completed two days before you make it. I would like to review it briefly with you. If you run into problems or have questions before then, please let me know.

1. Select work that represents your best effort and thinking during the semester. Try to select work with some variety. For example, choose one problem you have solved, one explanation of a mathematical idea, one project in which you contributed, or several exam questions.

2. Organize your work in a way that makes sense—from simple problems to difficult problems, from beginning of semester to end of semester, from short problems to long problems, from most liked to least liked.

3. Make an outline of what you plan to say. You will have only 30 minutes for your presentation, so be efficient and to the point in your explanations. Decide what you will highlight in presenting each piece of work.

4. Review each piece of work carefully and make sure you understand it. Remember, you completed some of the work several months ago.

5. Anticipate questions your parents might ask you about your work. What mathematics questions might they ask? Why have you chosen this work? Why is this topic important? What did you like most about math class this year?

Good luck. Make sure your parents or family are proud of your work and presentation.

Exemplary Mathematics Assessment Tasks for Grades 9–12

House of Cards

The house of cards in **figure 5.1** is 3 stories high, and 15 cards are needed.

How many cards would be needed for a similar house 10 stories high?

The world record for the greatest number of stories is 61. How many cards would you need to break this record and make a house 62 stories high?

FIG. 5.1

HOUSE OF CARDS

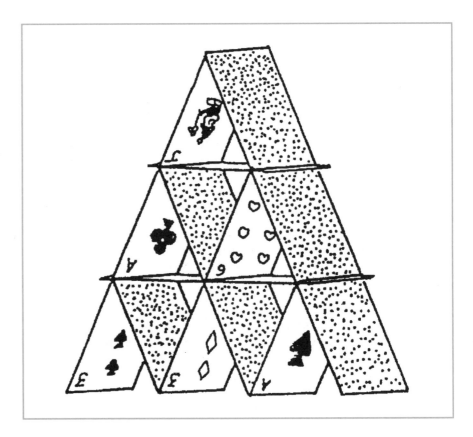

This material is adapted from *Problems with Patterns and Numbers*, originally published by the Shell Centre for Mathematical Education at Nottingham University, England. This and other Shell products are now available from QED of York (England) at +44-1904-424242 and qed@enterprise.net.

Skeleton Tower

Look at the tower in **figure 5.2**.

FIG. 5.2

SKELETON TOWER

▪ How many cubes are needed to build this tower?

▪ How many cubes are needed to build a tower like this, but 12 cubes high?

▪ Explain how you worked out your answer to the first question.

▪ How would you calculate the number of cubes needed for a tower *n* cubes high?

This material is adapted from *Problems with Patterns and Numbers*, originally published by the Shell Centre for Mathematical Education at Nottingham University, England. This and other Shell products are now available from QED of York (England) at +44-1904-424242 and qed@enterprise.net.

Bucket of Water

FIG. 5.3

WATER AND PERCENT GRAPH

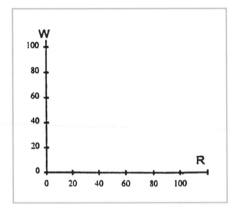

I have some water in a bucket. The water weighs 99 kilograms and the bucket weighs one kilogram.

1. What percent of the total weight of the water and the bucket is the water?

2. If 5 kilograms of water is removed, what percent of the total weight of the water and the bucket is the water? [Express your answer to the nearest tenth of a percent.]

3. How many kilograms of water must be removed from the bucket so that the weight of the remaining water is 95% of the total combined weight of the water and the bucket?

4. How many kilograms of water must be removed from the bucket so that the weight of the remaining water is 50% of the total combined weight of the water and the bucket?

5. Suppose the desired percent is R and the amount of water that needs to be removed is W. Find an equation that shows a relationship between R and W.

6. Sketch a graph of the equation on the graph in **figure 5.3**.

7. Is it possible to reduce the percentage of water to 1% of the combined weight of the water and bucket? Provide a reason for your answer.

Developed by William E. Campbell for the Exeter Mathematics Institute. Reprinted with permission from William Campbell and Exeter Academy.

CHAPTER 5

Paper Cups

Figure 5.4 below shows drawings of one paper cup and six paper cups that have been "stacked" together. [The cups are shown half size.]

1. What is the height in centimeters of one full size cup?

2. When the cups are "stacked," by how much distance does each cup stick up beyond the one below?

3. What would the total height of 20 stacked cups be?

4. How many cups would fit in a space one meter high?

5. Create a rule that gives the height of a stack of cups in terms of the number of cups in the stack. Define your variables and tell how you created your rule.

FIG. 5.4

PAPER CUP STACKS

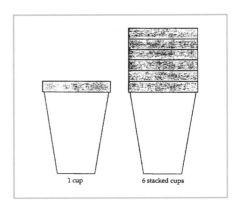

1 cup   6 stacked cups

All Sports Season Ticket Sales

Maximum Price for Package	Total Number Willing to Pay This Price
$50	765
$75	620
$90	540
$95	495
$115	410
$135	290
$150	210
$175	150

Your school wants to boost interest in its athletic program. It has decided to sell a pass that will allow the ticket holder to attend all athletic events at the school. The 811 families in the community with students in the school were surveyed and asked the question, "What is the most you would pay for an all sports season ticket package?" The results of the survey are given to the left.

Use the data to determine the optimal ticket price.

Contemporary Precalculus through Application. Chicago: Everyday Learning Corporation, 1999

CHAPTER 5

Wiggie Growth

A new insect has been discovered in Texas! They are lively little creatures called Wiggies. They reproduce asexually (by themselves). Reproduction is triggered when the underside of the Wiggie is exposed to light. You have found a population of three Wiggies living outside the school in an old dead tree. Simulate the reproduction process of these three Wiggies with the following experiment:

1. Place three Skittles, each representing the three Wiggies in your original population, into a flat container with a lid. Consider the "s" side of the Skittle to be the underside of the Wiggie.

2. Shake the container, open the top, and count the number of "s" marks you can see. Add another Skittle for each "s" showing (representing a new Wiggie that has been produced). Using the table in **figure 5.5**, record the number of Wiggies in the container as being the number alive after the first reproductive cycle. (Assume that no Wiggies have died.)

3. Shake the container again, remove the lid, and count the number of "s" marks showing. Add another Skittle for each "s" showing and record the number as the total population of Wiggies at the end of the second reproductive cycle.

4. Repeat this process for two more shakes and record the results each time.

5. Make a guess as to what the population of Wiggies would be after 8 more shakes (a total of 12 shakes).

6. Continue the process until you have completed 12 shakes or have run out of Skittles. Be sure to record your results each time in the table in **figure 5.5**.

7. Make a scatterplot of the data. What do you notice? What would you predict for 24 shakes? Why?

Adapted from a task by William E. Campbell for the Exeter Mathematics Institute. Reprinted with permission from William Campbell and Exeter Academy.

FIG. 5.5

WIGGIES TABLE

reproduction cycle	total population of Wiggies
0	3
1	
2	
3	
4	
5	
6	
7	
8	
9	
10	
11	
12	

Paper Folding

1. How many times is it possible to fold a piece of paper? Take an 8 1/2″ × 11″ sheet of paper and fold it in half. You now have something that is two pages thick. Fold that piece in half again. How thick is it now? Continue folding and record your results in the second column in **figure 5.6** up to six folds.

FIG. 5.6

PAPER-FOLDING CHART

number of folds	thickness in pages	thickness in inches
1	2	0.006
2	4	
3		
4		
5		
6		

2. If one piece of paper is 0.003 inches thick, how thick would two pages be? How thick would four pages be? Record the thickness in inches in the third column of your table for up to six folds.

3. If it were possible to fold the paper 15 times, determine the thickness in pages that your paper stack would have. Record your results in the blank row of your table. Now compute the number of inches this stack formed from 15 folds and record it in column three.

4. From your work thus far, how thick in feet would you estimate that a stack formed by 25 folds would be? Write your estimate below. Now compute the actual thickness of the stack formed by 25 folds.

    Estimate _____ Actual _____

5. Write a formula that gives the thickness *in feet* of the folded paper as a function of the number of folds.

6. Mount Everest, the tallest mountain in the world, is 29,028 feet high. About how many folds would it take to match this height?

7. The moon is 286,000 miles away. How many folds would it take to form a stack that would reach the moon?

CHAPTER 5

Developed by William E. Campbell for the Exeter Mathematics Institute. Reprinted with permission from William Campbell and Exeter Academy.

The Golf Shot

The height (in feet) above the ground of a golf ball depends on the time, t, (in seconds) it has been in flight. A golfer has hit a shot off the tee that has a height given approximately by $h = 80t - 16t^2$.

a. Sketch a graph of this function on the graph in **figure 5.7**:

FIG. 5.7

GRAPH OF GOLF SHOT

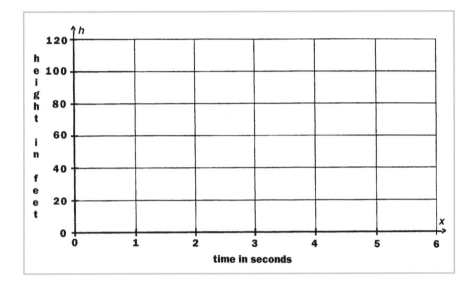

b. Answer the following questions:

- What time does the golf ball land on the ground?
- What is the maximum height of the ball?
- How long after it is hit does the golf ball reach that height?
- What is the height of the ball at 3.5 seconds?
- At about what time is the ball first 60 feet in the air?
- Is it 60 feet high a second time? If so, when?

c. Suppose the same golfer hit a second ball from a tee that was elevated 20 feet above the fairway.

- What effect would that have on the value of your table?
- Write a function that describes the new path of the ball.
- Sketch the new relationship between height and time on your graph above.
- What time will this second golf ball land on the ground?
- What is the maximum height of the ball?
- How long after it is hit does the golf ball reach that maximum height?

Adapted from a task by William E. Campbell for the Exeter Mathematics Institute. Reprinted with permission from William Campbell and Exeter Academy.

Tree Growth

1. A black cherry tree seedling is planted in the middle of a field. The black cherry grows rapidly as long as it is not in the shade. Scientists have examined the growth of black cherry trees over periods of time and have found that their growth is modeled by this equation:

    $h = 100e^{.03t} - 70$, where t is the number of years since the tree was planted and h is the height of the tree in centimeters.

   - How old is the tree when the height is 4 meters? When it is 8 meters? 12 meters? 16 meters?

   - Examine the height of the tree when time is increasing. Explain the pattern.

   - Develop an alternative algebraic representation of the age of the tree with respect to its height.

   - Graph the original equation and your new equation. What observations can you make about the two graphs? Justify your statement using algebra or a definition, theorem, and so on.

2. At the same time that the black cherry tree is planted, an 18-meter sugar maple tree is growing in the woods. The sugar maple grows in the shade, but at a slow rate. Scientists have determined that the sugar maple tree grows according to a logarithmic model. Sketch a graph of the sugar maple tree's growth, labeling relevant information. Write an explanation to justify your graph.

3. Using the information from 1 and 2, analyze the advantages and limitations of the different models.

CHAPTER 5

Orchard Observer

An orchard is planted in a rectangular grid such as the one seen in figure 5.8. The trees are all evenly spaced along rows and columns. You, the observer, are sitting in a swivel chair at point *O*. As you swing around in your chair, is there any line of sight along which you see no trees? [Assume the grid continues infinitely to the right and up.]

Consider the grid to be the first quadrant of a coordinate axis system. You, the observer, are at (0,0) and the trees are located by coordinates that are nonzero integers. Thus the trees in the first row are at (1,1), (2,1), (3,1), . . . , the second row at (1,2), (2,2), . . . , and so forth.

1. List the coordinates of four trees that you can see.

2. List the coordinates of four trees that you cannot see because they are hidden by other trees.

3. Can you see trees at the following locations? (5,3), (6,3), (6,8), (2,10), (2,15), (18,24)

4. List some trees hidden by the tree at (1,2).

5. What characterizes the coordinates of trees hidden by a given tree?

6. What characterizes the coordinates of trees that you can see?

7. Return to the original questions. Are there any openings through which you can see no trees no matter how large a forest we consider? Explain your answer.

Developed by William E. Campbell for the Exeter Mathematics Institute. Reprinted with permission from William Campbell and Exeter Academy.

FIG. 5.8

ORCHARD

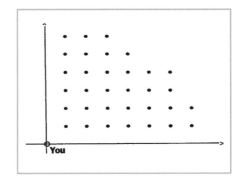

Graphs and Tables

1. Without plotting, choose the best sketch of a graph from graphs (a) through (l) in **figure 5.10** to fit each of the tables in **figure 5.9**. Particular graphs may fit more than one table. Copy the most suitable graph for each, name the axes clearly, and explain your choice. If you cannot find the graph you want, draw your own version.

FIG. 5.9

TABLES

1. Cooling Coffee

Time (minutes)	0	5	10	15	20	25	30
Temperature (C°)	90	79	70	62	55	49	44

2. Cooking Times for Turkey

Weight (lb)	6	8	10	12	14	16	18	20
Time (hours)	2½	3	3½	4	4½	5	5½	6

3. How a Baby Grew Before Birth

Age (months)	2	3	4	5	6	7	8	9
Length (cm)	4	9	16	24	30	34	38	42

4. After Three Pints of Beer . . .

Time (hours)	1	2	3	4	5	6	7
Alcohol in the blood (mg/100ml)	90	75	60	45	30	15	0

5. Number of Bird Species on a Volcanic Island

Year	1880	1890	1900	1910	1920	1930	1940
Number of Species	0	1	5	17	30	30	30

6. Life Expectancy

Age (years)	Number of Survivors	Age (years)	Number of Survivors
0	1000	50	913
5	979	60	808
10	978	70	579
20	972	80	248
30	963	90	32
40	950	100	1

CHAPTER *5*

2. Make up tables of numbers that will correspond to the graphs (m) through (r) in **figure 5.11**.

3. Make up some tables on your own, and sketch the corresponding graphs on a separate sheet of paper. Pass only the tables to another student. Ask him or her to sketch the graphs from your tables. Compare his or her solutions with yours.

FIG. 5.11

SKETCHES OF GRAPHS

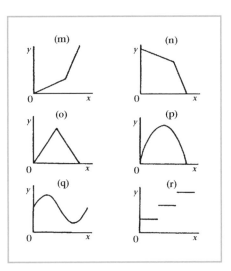

FIG. 5.10

SKETCHES OF GRAPHS

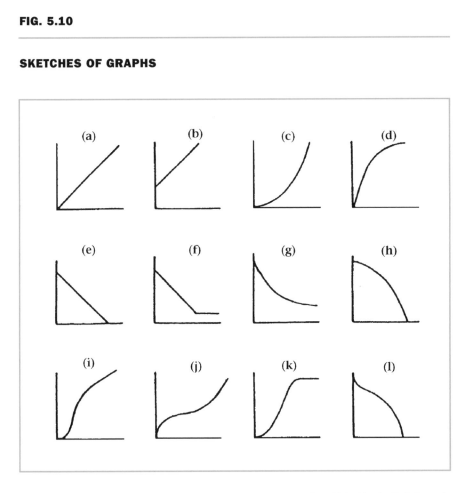

This material is adapted from *The Language of Functions and Graphs*, originally published by the Shell Centre for Mathematical Education at Nottingham University, England. This and other Shell products are now available from QED of York (England) at +44-1904-424242 and qed@enterprise.net.

Height-Volume Graphs

FIG. 5.12

BEAKERS X, A, B

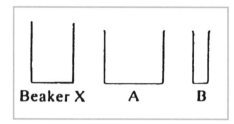

Beaker X   A   B

In order to calibrate a bottle so that it can be used to measure liquids, it is necessary to know how the height of the liquid depends on the volume in the bottle. The graph in **figure 5.12** shows how the height of liquid in beaker X varies as water is steadily dripped into it. Copy the graph, and *on the same diagram*, show the height-volume relationship for beakers A and B.

Sketch two more graphs for beakers C and D, illustrated in **figure 5.13**.

Sketch two more graphs for beakers E and F, illustrated in **figure 5.14**.

Below are six bottles in **figure 5.15** and nine graphs in **figure 5.16**. Choose the correct graph for each bottle. Explain your reasoning clearly. For the remaining three graphs, sketch what the bottles should look like.

FIG. 5.13

BEAKERS C AND D

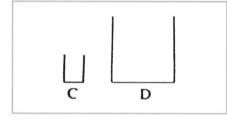

C   D

FIG. 5.14

BEAKERS E AND F

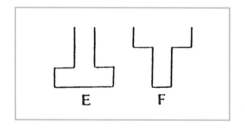

E   F

FIG. 5.15

SIX BOTTLES

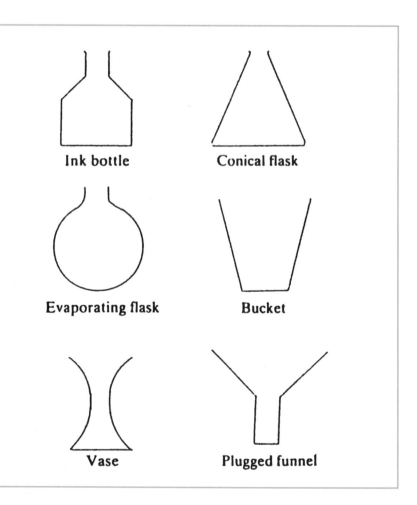

Ink bottle   Conical flask

Evaporating flask   Bucket

Vase   Plugged funnel

Sketch graphs for the following sequence of bottles in figure 5.17.

Using your sketches, explain why a bottle with straight sloping sides does not give a straight-line graph (i.e., explain why the ink bottle does not correspond to the graph in **fig. 5.10g**).

Invent your own bottles and sketch their graphs on a separate sheet of paper. Pass only the graphs to another student. Can he or she reconstruct the shape of the original bottles using only your graphs? If not, try to discover what errors are being made.

Is it possible to draw two different bottles that give the same height-volume graph? Try to draw some examples.

This material is adapted from *The Language of Functions and Graphs*, originally published by the Shell Centre for Mathematical Education at Nottingham University, England. This and other Shell products are now available from QED of York (England) at +44-1904-424242 and qed@enterprise.net.

FIG. 5.17

SEQUENCE OF BOTTLES

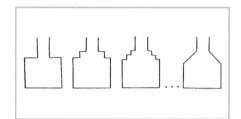

FIG. 5.16

NINE GRAPHS

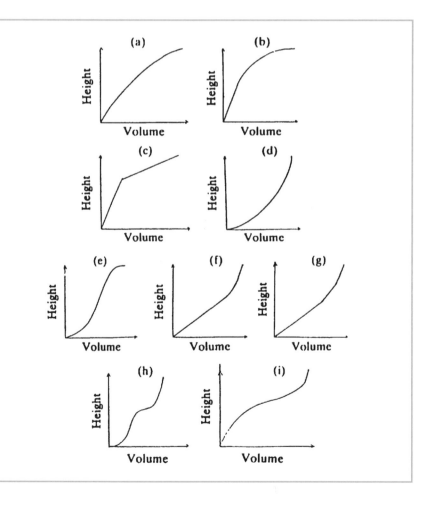

The Hurdles Race

The rough sketch graph in **figure 5.18** describes what happens when three athletes A, B, and C enter a 400-meter hurdles race. Imagine that you are the race commentator. Describe (in writing) what is happening as carefully as you can. You do not need to measure anything accurately.

FIG. 5.18

THE HURDLES RACE GRAPH

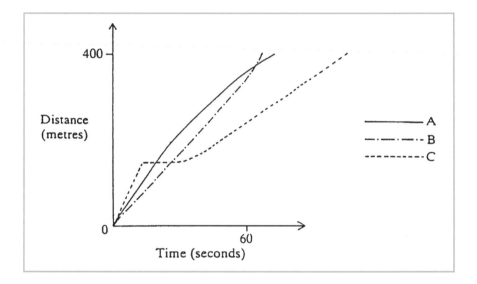

This material is adapted from *The Language of Functions and Graphs*, originally published by the Shell Centre for Mathematical Education at Nottingham University, England. This and other Shell products are now available from QED of York (England) at +44-1904-424242 and qed@enterprise.net.

Calendar Patterns

Figure 5.19 shows a calendar for June 1997.

1. Pick any number under Sunday and any number under Thursday and add them together. In what column is the answer? [You can extend the calendar to as many days as you need.] Try two other numbers, again one from Sunday and one from Thursday. Is the result the same? Is this true no matter what two numbers from these two days are chosen? Explain your answer.

2. Pick any Wednesday number and any number from Saturday. Multiply the two numbers together. Under what day does your answer appear? Try it again. Show why this might happen every time.

3. Make up some other relationships that would hold for numbers chosen from selected days. Give reasons why your relationships hold.

4. Select any 3 × 3 group of numbers from the calendar [for example, 1, 2, 3, 8, 9, 10, 15, 16, 17] and put a box around them. Add the three numbers along any straight line drawn through the center number. What do you notice? Try another 3 × 3 group of numbers. What generalizations can you make?

Developed by William E. Campbell for the Exeter Mathematics Institute. Reprinted with permission from William Campbell and Exeter Academy.

FIG.5.19

JUNE 1997 CALENDAR

Sun.	Mon.	Tue.	Wed.	Thu.	Fri.	Sat.
1	2	3	4	5	6	7
8	9	10	11	12	13	14
15	16	17	18	19	20	21
22	23	24	25	26	27	28
29	30					

The Box Investigation

FIG. 5.20

CUT CORNERS

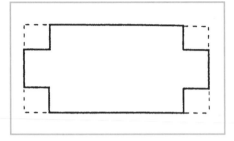

FIG. 5.21

BOX FOLDS

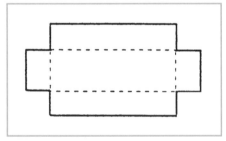

FIG. 5.22

TABLE OF VOLUMES

size of cut	volume of box
0 cm	
1 cm	
2 cm	
3 cm	
4 cm	
5 cm	
6 cm	
7 cm	
8 cm	
9 cm	

1. Take a sheet of graph paper that is 18 cm wide and 24 cm long.

2. Cut a 1-cm square from each corner. Your paper should look like the picture in **figure 5.20**. The dotted lines outline the squares that were removed.

3. Crease your paper as accurately as possible along the four lines joining the cuts. The lines are dotted in **figure 5.21**.

4. Fold your paper along the creases and tape the sides to form a box without a top.

5. Compute the volume of the box in cubic units and record it in the appropriate space in the table in **figure 5.22**.

6. Collect the other data for the table by making other boxes from your sheet of paper. Make a scatterplot from your data. Make a guess about what type of equation might model these points.

7. Let the size of the cut be x centimeters. Imagine that you have cut out the squares and folded the box up. Represent the length, width, height, and volume of the box in terms of x.

8. What would be the size of the cut that would allow us to construct a box with maximum volume? What would the maximum volume of the box be?

Adapted from a task by William E. Campbell for the Exeter Mathematics Institute. Reprinted with permission from William Campbell and Exeter Academy.

CHAPTER 5

Predator-Prey

Animals in the woods of Kentucky are dependent on one another for food. For example, one species—say, owls—are dependent on another species—say, mice—for food. In this example, we say that the food stream travels from mice to owls. We can create a matrix describing this food stream by using 0's and 1's. The matrix in **figure 5.23** shows how eight species labeled A through H relate to one another in the food stream. For example, a 1 in row A, column B means that the food stream flows from B to A, or that B is food for A.

FIG. 5.23

FOOD STREAM

FROM

TO

$$\begin{array}{c} \\ A \\ B \\ C \\ D \\ E \\ F \\ G \\ H \end{array} \begin{array}{c} \begin{array}{cccccccc} A & B & C & D & E & F & G & H \end{array} \\ \begin{pmatrix} 0 & 1 & 0 & 0 & 1 & 0 & 1 & 1 \\ 0 & 0 & 0 & 1 & 0 & 1 & 1 & 0 \\ 0 & 0 & 0 & 0 & 1 & 0 & 0 & 0 \\ 0 & 0 & 0 & 0 & 0 & 1 & 0 & 0 \\ 0 & 0 & 0 & 1 & 0 & 0 & 0 & 0 \\ 0 & 0 & 0 & 0 & 0 & 0 & 0 & 0 \\ 0 & 0 & 0 & 0 & 0 & 0 & 0 & 0 \\ 0 & 0 & 1 & 0 & 0 & 0 & 0 & 0 \end{pmatrix} \end{array}$$

1. Column A and rows F and G consist entirely of zeros. What does this say about these three animal species?

2. There are food streams traveling from G to B and from B to A. We will call this food chain $G - B - A$. What is the longest food chain in Kentucky?

3. Two species are each other's rival if they have at least one common prey. Name the rival pairs of predators in Kentucky.

4. A toxic substance has entered the environment. Some of the species absorb this substance. Their bodies do not break it down, so it enters the body of any predator that eats them and gets passed on again. Regardless of which species first comes in contact with the toxic substance, it will eventually reach species A. Show that this is true.

The Transmitting Tower

WKPC FM 99.9 in PreCalc City ran a preference survey in ten surrounding cities not yet included in its listening area. The survey showed that a substantial audience would be available in three of these areas— Nicholasville, located 300 miles north and 300 miles east of PreCalc City; Smitherton, 200 miles north and 100 miles west of PreCalc City; and Calc Just Around the Corners, located 50 miles south and 450 miles east of PreCalc City. WKPC's board of directors approved the bid submitted by Barnes & Company for the construction of a transmitting tower to service these three cities. Where should the building materials for the tower be sent with respect to PreCalc City? Justify the location of the construction site.

Developed by the teachers of Jessamine County High School in Nicholasville, Kentucky. Reprinted with their permission.

CHAPTER 5

Box It!

Box It! Company receives a rush order to ship 500 boxes without lids. The boxes must hold more than three cubic feet. The company has an extra supply of 5' × 3' sheets of cardboard on hand. You are the company's on-site mathematician. Your task is to send a directive to the machine operators on how to set the machine to produce boxes with the minimum amount of waste. You are also required to send a full report to the vice-president of operations showing all details required to enable you to make the directive.

Developed by the teachers of Jessamine County High School in Nicholasville, Kentucky. Reprinted with their permission.

Disc-Ness

FIG. 5.24

PICTURE OF CYLINDERS

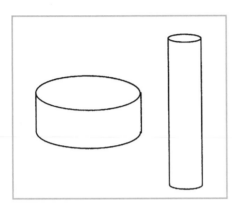

A coin is a disc, and an uncooked piece of spaghetti is a cylinder. If you think about it, however, a coin is also a cylinder and an uncooked piece of spaghetti is also a disc. Clearly the coin is more disc-like and the spaghetti is more cylinder-like.[See **fig. 5.24**.]

1. Given a coin, a tuna-fish can, and a soup can: Devise a definition of disc-ness that allows you to say which object is the most disc-like and which is the least.

2. Given a cardboard tube, a straw, and a piece of uncooked spaghetti: Use your definition of disc-ness to determine which object is the most disc-like and which is the least.

3. Write a formula (or algorithm or algebraic sentence) which expresses your measure of disc-ness. You may introduce any labels and definitions you like and use all the mathematical language you care to.

4. Make any measurements you need, and calculate a numerical value of disc-ness for each of the six items.

5. Do these numbers seem reasonable in light of your notion of disc-ness?

6. How would you change your answers to these questions if you were asked to write a formula for cylinder-ness rather than disc-ness?

From *Balanced Assessment for the Mathematics Curriculum: Advanced High School Assessment Package 1* by Alan Schoenfeld, Hugh Burkhardt, Phil Daro, Jim Ridgway, Judah Schwartz and Sandra Wilcox; copyright © 1999 by the Regents of the University of California. Reprinted with permission from Dale Seymour Publications.

CHAPTER 5

Don't Fence Me In

A pony is standing still on a long straight road. The road surface is such that the pony can move along the road at 5 miles per hour.

On one side of the road is a grassy area through which the pony can travel at 4 miles per hour. Running along the other side of the road is wooded terrain through which the pony can travel at 3 miles per hour. [See **fig. 5.25**.]

FIG. 5.25

DON'T FENCE ME IN PICTURE

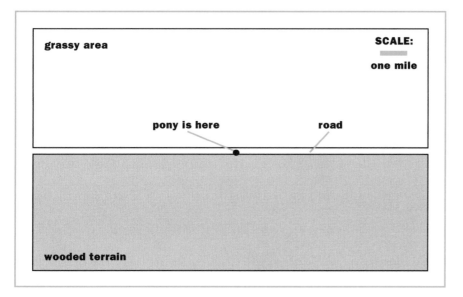

Suppose you want to erect a fence that would enclose all of the area that the pony can reach in an hour. (Ignore the width of the road.) Show where the fence would go if:

1. Once the pony starts in a given direction, it does not change direction. (Show the fence with a solid line.)

2. The pony moves freely. (Show the fence with a dotted line.)

In each case, explain your answer.

RESOURCES

NCTM

Bibliography

SOURCES FOR ASSESSMENT TASKS

Balanced Assessment Project. *High School* and *Advanced High School Packages*. White Plains, N.Y.: Dale Seymour Publications, 1999.

Herr, Ted, and Ken Johnson. *Problem Solving Strategies: Crossing the River with Dogs*. Berkeley, Calif.: Key Curriculum Press, 1994.

Kentucky Department of Education. *KIRIS Open-Ended Response Items*. Available on Web site: www.kde.state.ky.us/default.asp?m=13.

Mason, John. *Learning and Doing Mathematics*. Originally published by the Open University and now available from QED of York (England) at 44-1904-424242 and qed@enterprise.net.

New Standards Project. Washington, D.C.: National Center on Education and the Economy. Web site: www.ncee.org.

Shell Centre for Mathematical Education. *The Language of Functions and Graphs*. Nottingham, England: University of Nottingham, 1985. Available from QED of York (England) at 44-1904-424242 and qed@enterprise.net.

———. *Patterns and Numbers*. Nottingham, England: University of Nottingham, 1985.

RESOURCES

REFERENCES

Asturias, Harold. "Using Students' Portfolios to Assess Mathematical Understanding." *Mathematics Teacher* 87 (December 1994): 698–701.

Bartels, Bobbye Hoffman. "Promoting Mathematics Connections with Concept Mapping." *Mathematics Teaching in the Middle School* 1 (November-December 1995): 542–49.

Belcher, Terri, Grace Dávila Coates, José Franco, and Karen Mayfield-Ingram. "Assessment and Equity." In *Multicultural and Gender Equity in the Mathematics Classroom: The Gift of Diversity*, 1997 Yearbook of the National Council of Teachers of Mathematics, edited by Janet Trentacosta, pp. 195–200. Reston, Va.: National Council of Teachers of Mathematics, 1997.

Burrill, Gail. "Data-Driven Mathematics: A Curriculm Strand for High School Mathematics." *Mathematics Teacher* 89 (September 1996): 460–65.

Bush, William S., ed. *Mathematics Assessment: Cases and Discussion Questions for Grades K–5*. Reston, Va.: National Council of Teachers of Mathematics, forthcoming.

———. *Mathematics Assessment: Cases and Discussion Questions for Grades 6–12*. Reston, Va.: National Council of Teachers of Mathematics, 1999.

Bush, William S., and Steve Leinward, eds. *Mathematics Assessment: A Practical Handbook for Grades 6–8*. Reston, Va.: National Council of Teachers of Mathematics, 1999.

California Mathematics Council. *They're Counting on Us*. Sacramento, Calif.: California Mathematics Council, 1995.

Chambers, Donald L. "Integrating Assessment and Instruction." In *Assessment in the Mathematics Classroom*, 1993 Yearbook of the National Council of Teachers of Mathematics, edited by Norman L. Webb, pp. 17–25. Reston, Va.: National Council of Teachers of Mathematics, 1993.

Charles, Randall, Frank Lester, and Phares O'Daffer. *How to Evaluate Progress in Problem Solving*. Reston, Va.: National Council of Teachers of Mathematics, 1987.

Clarke, David. *Assessment Alternatives in Mathematics*. Canberra, Australia: Curriculum Development Centre, 1988.

————. *Constructive Assessment in Mathematics: Practical Steps for Classroom Teachers*. Berkeley, Calif.: Key Curriculum Press, 1997.

————. "Quality Mathematics: How Can We Tell?" *Mathematics Teacher* 88 (April 1995): 326–28.

Clarke, Doug, and Linda Wilson. "Valuing What We See." *Mathematics Teacher* 87 (October 1994): 542–45.

Connolly, Paul, and Teresa Vilardi, eds. *Writing to Learn Mathematics and Science*. New York: Teachers College Press, 1989.

Countryman, Joan. *Writing to Learn Mathematics: Strategies That Work*. Portsmouth, N.H.: Heinemann, 1992.

Coxford, Arthur F., James T. Fey, Christian R. Hirsch, Harold L. Schoen, Gail Burrill, Eric W. Hart, Ann E. Watkins, Mary Jo Messenger, and Beth Ritsema. *Contemporary Mathematics in Context: A Unified Approach*. Chicago: Everyday Learning Corp., 1998.

Crowley, Mary L. "Student Mathematics Portfolio: More than a Display Case." *Mathematics Teacher* 86 (October 1993): 544–47.

Cuevas, Gilbert J. "Developing Communication Skills in Mathematics for Students with Limited English Proficiency." *Mathematics Teacher* 84 (March 1991): 186–89.

Curcio, Frances R., and Alice F. Artzt. "Assessing Students' Ability to Analyze Data: Reaching beyond Computation." *Mathematics Teacher* 89 (November 1996): 668–73.

Edgerton, Richard T. "Applying the Curriculum Standards with Project Questions." *Mathematics Teacher* 86 (November 1993): 686–89.

Elliott, Wanda Leigh. "Writing: A Necessary Tool for Learning." *Mathematics Teacher* 89 (February 1996): 92–94.

Gay, Susan, and Margaret Thomas. "Just Because They Got It Right, Does It Mean They Know It?" In *Assessment in the Mathematics Classroom*, 1993 Yearbook of the National Council of Teachers of Mathematics, edited by Norman L. Webb, pp. 130–34. Reston, Va.: National Council of Teachers of Mathematics, 1993.

Kenney, Patricia Ann, and Edward A. Silver. "Student Self-Assessment in Mathematics." In *Assessment in the Mathematics Classroom,* 1993 Yearbook of the National Council of Teachers of Mathematics, edited by Norman L. Webb, pp. 229–38. Reston, Va.: National Council of Teachers of Mathematics, 1993.

Kern, Cherlyn. "Descriptive-Paragraph Miniproject." *Mathematics Teacher* 90 (May 1997): 362–63.

Khisty, Lena Licón. "Making Mathematics Accessible to Latino Students: Rethinking Instructional Practice." In *Multicultural and Gender Equity in the Mathematics Classroom: The Gift of Diversity*, 1997 Yearbook of the National Council of Teachers of Mathematics, edited by Janet Trentacosta, pp. 92–101. Reston, Va.: National Council of Teachers of Mathematics, 1997.

Kroll, Diana Lambdin, Joanne O. Masingila, and Sue Tinsley Mau. "Grading Cooperative Problem Solving." *Mathematics Teacher* 85 (November 1992): 619–27.

Kuhs, Therese M. "Portfolio Assessment: Making It Work for the First Time." *Mathematics Teacher* 87 (May 1994): 332–35.

Lambdin, Diana V., and Clare Forseth. "Seamless Assessment/Instruction = Good Teaching." *Teaching Children Mathematics* 2 (January 1996): 294–98.

LeGere, Adele. "Collaboration and Writing in the Mathematics Classroom." *Mathematics Teacher* 84 (March 1991): 166–71.

Manon, John Rahn. "The Mathematics Test: A New Role for an Old Friend." *Mathematics Teacher* 88 (February 1995): 138–41.

Mathematical Sciences Education Board. *Everybody Counts: A Report to the Nation on the Future of Mathematics Education*. Washington, D.C.: National Academy Press, 1989.

———. *Measuring What Counts: A Conceptual Guide for Mathematics Assessment*. Washington, D.C.: National Academy Press, 1993.

Mayer, Jennifer, and Susan Hillman. "Assessing Students' Thinking through Writing." *Mathematics Teacher* 89 (May 1996): 428–32.

McIntosh, Margaret E. "No Time for Writing in Your Class?" *Mathematics Teacher* 84 (September 1991): 423–33.

Merseth, Katherine K., and Joan Karp. *Cases of Secondary Mathematics Classrooms*. Cambridge: Harvard Case Development Project, forthcoming.

Miller, L. Diane. "Begin Mathematics Class with Writing." *Mathematics Teacher* 85 (May 1992): 354–55.

———. "Writing to Learn Mathematics." *Mathematics Teacher* 84 (October 1991): 516–21.

National Council of Teachers of Mathematics. *Assessment Standards for School Mathematics*. Reston, Va.: National Council of Teachers of Mathematics, 1995.

———. *Curriculum and Evaluation Standards for School Mathematics*. Reston, Va.: National Council of Teachers of Mathematics, 1989.

———. *Professional Standards for Teaching Mathematics*. Reston, Va.: National Council of Teachers of Mathematics, 1991.

Public Broadcasting Service. *PBS MATHLINE*. Alexandria, Va.: Public Broadcasting Service, 1994.

Pugalee, David K. "Connecting Writing to the Mathematics Curriculum." *Mathematics Teacher* 90 (April 1997): 308–10.

Robinson, Donita. "Student Portfolios in Mathematics." *Mathematics Teacher* 91 (April 1998): 318–25.

Sammons, Kay B., Beth Kobett, Joan Heiss, and Francis (Skip) Fennell. "Linking Instruction and Assessment in the Mathematics Classroom." *Arithmetic Teacher* 39 (February 1992): 11–16.

Schloemer, Cathy G. "Aligning Assessment with the NCTM's Curriculum Standards." *Mathematics Teacher* 86 (December 1993): 722–25.

———. "Some Practical Possibilities for Alternative Assessment." *Mathematics Teacher* 90 (January 1997): 46–49.

RESOURCES

Shimizu, Yoshinori, and Diana V. Lambdin. "Assessing Students' Performance on an Extended Problem-Solving Task: A Story from a Japanese Classroom." *Mathematics Teacher* 90 (November 1997): 658–64.

Shute, William, William Shirk, and George Porter. *Solid Geometry*. New York: American Book Co., 1957.

Socha, Susan. "Questions with Multiple Answers." *Mathematics Teacher* 84 (November 1991): 638–40.

Stenmark, Jean Kerr, ed. *Mathematics Assessment: Myths, Models, Good Questions, and Practical Suggestions*. Reston, Va.: National Council of Teachers of Mathematics, 1991.

Stenmark, Jean Kerr, Pam Beck, and Harold Asturias. "A Room with More than One View*." Mathematics Teaching in the Middle School* 1 (April 1994): 44–49.

Stiggins, Richard J. *Student-Centered Classroom Assessment*. New York: Macmillan College Publishing, 1994.

Swan, Malcolm. "Assessing Mathematical Processes: The English Experience." *Mathematics Teaching in the Middle School* 1 (March-April 1996): 706–11.

Thompson, Denisse R., Charlene E. Beckman, and Sharon L. Senk. "Improving Classroom Tests as a Means of Improving Assessment." *Mathematics Teacher* 90 (January 1997): 58–64.

Vincent, Mary Lynn, and Linda Wilson. "Informal Assessment: A Story from the Classroom." *Mathematics Teacher* 89 (March 1996): 248–50.

WGBH Educational Foundation. *Assessment Library for Grades K–12*. Boston: WGBH Educational Foundation, 1998.

Wiggins, Grant. "Honesty and Fairness: Toward Better Grading and Reporting." In *Communicating Student Learning,* 1996 Yearbook of the Association for Supervision and Curriculum Development, edited by Thomas Gushey, pp. 141–77. Alexandria, Va.: Association for Supervision and Curriculum Development, 1996.

BIBLIOGRAPHY

Wilcox, Sandra, and Perry Lanier. *Using Assessment to Reshape Teaching: A Casebook for Teachers and Teacher Educators, Curriculum and Staff Development Specialists*. Hillsdale, N.J.: Lawrence Erlbaum Associates, forthcoming.

Wilcox, Sandra K., and Ronald S. Zielinski. "Using the Assessment of Students' Learning to Reshape Teaching." *Mathematics Teacher* 90 (March 1997): 223–29.

Zawojewski, Judith S. "Polishing a Data Task: Seeing Better Assessment." *Teaching Children Mathematics* 2 (February 1996): 372–78.

Zawojewski, Judith S., and Richard Lesh. "Scores and Grades: What Are the Problems? What Are the Alternatives?" *Mathematics Teaching in the Middle School* 1 (May 1996): 776–79.

RESOURCES

RESOURCES

Index